Thank you for your purchase. To see our other books, please visit our website at www.danielleadams.com.

Published by :
~ THE DANIELLE ADAMS PUBLISHING CO. ~
BOX 100 ☆ MERION STATION, PA 19066
FAX 610/642-6832 ☆ VOICE 610/642-1000
©2012

The Danielle Adams Publishing Company
Post Office Box 100
Merion Station, PA 19066

Published by
The Danielle Adams Publishing Company
Post Office Box 100
Merion Station, PA 19066
Visit www.danielleadams.com

ISBN 10 digit: 0-9792924-5-x
ISBN 13 digit: 978-0-9792924-5-3
Copyright 2012 · All Rights Reserved

LIFE'S TOO SHORT

To Dance with Ugly Women

A Man's Collection of Jokes, One-Liners, Sayings,
and Quotes… about Women

Edited and Compiled by Dr. Manly Mann

Jokes

Every woman has a secret desire to write checks.

Give a woman an inch, and she thinks she's a ruler.

"I could hug you till you break," he said passionately, and gave her a big squeeze, until he felt her crack.

A man is as old as the woman he feels.

If you want to know why they're called the opposite sex, express an opinion!

She's one of 5 million overweight women. These, of course, are round figures.

"Carry your bag, sir?"
"No, let her walk!"

"What do you do when a woman faints?"
Dr. Mann: "I stop Kissing Her!"

Show Me Your Tits!

Why is a fat girl like a moped?
They're both fun to ride till a friend sees you!

If your wife wants to learn to drive,
don't stand in her way.

Wife: An attachment you screw on the bed
to get the housework done.

Foreplay is optional

"It's only the third quarter - you should order
another couple of pitchers."

Quotations

Here's to women, if we could only fall into
their arms without falling into their hands.
Ambrose Bierce
Quotations about Women   165

A woman is only a woman, but a good cigar
is a smoke.
Rudyard Kipling
More Quotations about Women   169

If a woman likes another woman, she's cordial.
If she doesn't like her, she's very cordial.
Irvin S. Cobb
Still More Quotes About Women   175

Let us have wine and women, mirth and lafter,
sermons and soda water the day after.
Lord Byron
Some people like women   179

Quotations About Women, continued...

Men, some to pleasure, some to business take,
but every woman is at heart a rake.
Alexander Pope
Some people don't like women   181

Next to the wound, what women make best
is the bandage. *Barbey d'Aurevilly*
Some people have mixed feelings   183

A true gentlemen is one who is never
unintentionally rude. *Oscar Wilde*
Sayings about Men   187

When thou goest to woman, take thy whip.
Friedrich Nietzsche
These people are tough on women 191

All tragedies are finished by a death,
All comedies are ended by a marriage.
Lord Byron
Quotations about Marriage   195

In the election of a wife as in a project of war,
to err but once is to be undone forever.
Thomas Middleton
Quotations about Wives   201

Apparently, the way to a girl's heart is
to saw her in half. *Victor Mature*
Famous People Quotations 203

You call this a party? The beer is warm
and the women are cold! *Groucho Marx*
Movie Quotations about Women   207

The years that a woman subtracts from her age
are not lost. They are added onto the ages of
other women. *Deane de Poitiers*
Quotes from Women, on Women 213

Never trust a woman who tells her real age.
A woman who would tell one that would tell
one anything. *Oscar Wilde*
Advice   219

A woman always has her revenge ready.
Moliere Warningser   **Warnings   223**

LIFE'S TOO SHORT
TO DANCE WITH UGLY WOMEN…

HAVE FUN!

Every woman has a secret desire to write checks.

Sayings about Women

Behind every successful man is a woman... who wants a mink coat.

Even if you can't read a girl like a book, it's nice to thumb through the pages.

Nothing makes a girl so beautiful as a few drinks!

Whoever named them the fairer sex was a poor judge of justice.

When with a woman eat, drink and be wary.

Few things are more expensive than a girl who is free for the evening.

She's not too difficult to find - just open your wallet and there she is!

You can always tell when a woman is looking for a husband - she is either single or married.

Any woman who says she is going to meet you half way is usually a poor judge of distance.

Legs are a girls best friend, but even best friends must part.

Every man has his woman, but the iceman has his pick.

You can't kiss a girl unexpectedly - only sooner than she thought!

A lawyer is a person who will stay up all night trying to break a girl's will.

The reason women live longer than men is they have no wives.

The more I know about women, the more I like my dog.

Many a poor man was once a rich bachelor.

If a good girl can't be led into temptation, what is she good for?

When dictating to your secretary, always end a sentence with a proposition.

Study meteorology - so you can look in a woman's eyes and tell whether.

Most women are better if you treat them to rum and coax.

The best way to fight a woman is with a hat. Grab it and run!

Joint bank accounts prove most women are quick on the draw.

Some women carry their age well because they have years of experience.

She may not want to marry you for your money, but she may not know any other way to get it.

Women are like tea bags - you don't know their full strength until they are in hot water.

Girls shouldn't be allowed to study foreign languages - one tounge is enough for any woman.

Man's troubles are due to three things: Women, money, and both!

Running after a woman never did anybody any harm. It's the catching them that does all the damage.

Behind every famous man is a woman who says there is a woman behind every famous man.

Two kinds of women - those who make a home for a man, and those who make a man for a home.

Legs like hers are few and far between.

Dear, how did you expect me to remember your birthday when you don't look a day older.

To all you fat ladies: a word to the wide should be sufficient.

There are some women who don't care for a man's company, unless they own it.

Most women are never satisfied - they are either trying to put on weight, take it off, or rearrange it.

To all you virgins: Thanks for nothing!

Give a women an inch and she thinks she's a ruler.

One and Two Liners About Women...

When two cars are double parked, the one parked by the woman is the one on the top.

There are two kinds of women - careless ones who lose their earrings, and careful ones who lose only one earring.

The only good thing you can say about fat women is that a lot of them have a good time.

She's a great after dinner speaker... when she speaks, she's usually after dinner.

Women are like a baseball umpires - they makes quick decisions, they never reverse any of them, and they don't think you're safe when you're out.

When a woman really loves a man he can make her do almost anything she really wants to do.

What's better than roses on your piano?
Two lips on your organ.

I had an argument with my new girlfriend -
she doesn't like the way I feel about her.

I came to see her off, and she certainly was.

Every man should know how to cook and
clean the house - just in case he can't find a
wife.

Some women cause happiness wherever
they go, some whenever they go.

I knew her 40 years ago and she still looks
the same as she does today. Old.

Some people say she looks like a million
and mean every year of it.

I knew some college girls poor in history
but great on dates.

Just before her birthday his friends asked him what he was getting for her. He said he wasn't refusing any reasonable offer.

Some women reach success by attireless effort.

She says she got that dress for a ridiculous figure. Obviously!

I made a new years resolution to cut down on wine and women. It was the worst afternoon of my life.

I went out with a insurance man's daughter because I liked her policy.

I could hug you till you break, he said passionately, and gave her a big squeeze, until he felt her crack.

More one and two liners:

Pills, rubbers, coils, foam - there's only one sure way to keep your wife from getting pregnant - get a good secretarial service.

Good times... bad times... with most women all that matters is the present.

Is the man who flirts with the waitress playing for bigger steaks?

When a woman loves her husband, he can make her do anything she wants to do.

I made up my mind to stay home but it was too late, she made up her face to go out.

A crazy woman went into a psychiatrist who told her she was crazy. "I want a second opinion." "O.K." said the Doc, "And you're ugly too."

Her vocabulary is small, but the turnover is terrific!

If a woman's intuition is so good, why do they ask so many questions.

Even if man could understand women, he still wouldn't believe it.

Her friends call her Channel 2 cause anyone can pick her up, especially late at night.

Does the fellow who sleeps with his sister in law have it in for his brother.

There was an old lady who lived in a shoe, she had so many children she could stretch her uterus around a rain barrel.

Love is like a poker game - it starts with a pair, she gets a flush, he shows diamonds, and ends with a full house, her holding clubs.

Did you hear Snow White woke up feeling a little grumpy?

The nice thing about dictating letters is that you can use a lot of words you don't know how to spell.

What do you call a woman with one foot? Eileen

What do you call a woman captured by cannibals? Candy

What do you call a woman with one leg? Peg

What do you call a woman lying on the beach? Sandi.

If a man is talking in the forest with no women around is he still wrong?

If you want to know why they're called the opposite sex, express an opinion.

More Sayings about Women!

Remember sleep is the best thing in the world, next to a woman.

Some women reduce and reduce, but never become a bargain.

So long as a women have curves, men can have angles.

Some women are not free for the night... but they are reasonable.

She says when she's down in the dumps she gets a new hat... Obviously, that's where she gets them.

Most women, when you invite them over after dinner - that's what they come after.

For a girl without principle, she draws considerable interest.

A girl's face may be her fortune, but other parts draw interest.

Women who dress to kill usually cook the same way.

At school she was voted most likely to concede.

Do women who are well reared look good from the front, also.

Women who marry a man for money usually divorce him for the same reason.

A fellow offered her a few drinks in his apartment and she reclined.

Some women are like an appendix - if you take them out once, that's enough!

She's always ready to go out for a little fund.

She brings out the animal in men - mink.

Her resistance at the start is not so much a proof of her virtue as her experience.

The perfect gentleman - holds open the door when his wife comes in with a bag of groceries.

He's waiting for the right girl to come alone.

They call him sailor because he likes to see a little port in every girl.

All he asks for in life is a little peach and quiet.

It's a lovely fur coat, but she's not saying how much she played for it.

A line that makes a girl popular is one of least resistance.

She can't add, but she certainly can distract.

She's a great deceptionist... When the little bell on her typewriter rings, she thinks its time for a coffee break.

He wanted only one single thing in life - himself.

She doesn't care for him at all, but she lives on his account.

Absence makes the heart go wander.

Did you lose your girlfriend because you can't remember where you laid her?

"You know dear, I've been thinking about our argument and well... I've decided you're right." "That won't help you at all," she replied. "I've changed my mind."

She's very mature... In fact, she's past due.

Modern girls like to wash their face and neck.

Women may be able to fake orgasms, but men can fake a whole relationship.

Men have two emotions, hungry and horny. If you see him without an erection, make him a sandwich.

A man is as old as the woman he feels.

Still More Sayings

Most women are not hard of hearing, just hard of listening.

A pretty girl is like a malady.

Some women won't play ball unless you furnish a diamond.

Careful grooming and smooth paint will take 20 years off a woman's age, but you can't fool a long flight of stairs.

The age of a woman is like the speedometer of a used car - you know it's set back, but you don't know how far.

Women are like eating mushrooms; you never know which ones are good for you until it's too late.

Woman may be a dime a dozen, but when you cut that number down to one, it starts costing you.

Women run their fingers through your hair because they're after your scalp.

Most women are very nice when they want.

There are several ways to handle a woman - unfortunately no man has ever discovered what they are.

Some women look younger without a bra - it draws all the wrinkles out of their face.

She was so fat, when she wore a bathing suit the harpoon marks showed!

Women's breasts are like electric trains - originally meant for children, but it's the fathers that play with them mostly.

She was a farmer's daughter who couldn't keep her calves together.

She had a lovely figure ... but no one could meet it.

Then there was the sleepy bride who was so tired she couldn't wake up for a second.

I know a nearsighted girl who can't tell her friends until they're right on top of her.

She had her head examined, but they couldn't find anything.

They call her a broker - because after you meet her you are.

Men wake up as good-looking
  as they went to bed.
Women somehow
  deteriorate during the night.

I saw a woman wearing a sweatshirt that said "Guess" on it, so I said "Implants?"

The last fight was my fault - my wife asked "What's on TV?" I said, "Dust!"

She's one of 5 million overweight women.
These, of course, are round figures.

Just Jokes

I use a crank to start my car... and she drives
me to work, too.

—

A crazy woman went into a psychiatrist
who told her she was crazy. I want a second
opinion. "OK," said the Doc, "And you're ugly,
too."

—

She was always complaining I never gave
her anything so I gave her a girdle... that ought
to hold her!

—

My wife was complaining that I never listen
to her... or something like that.

They now make a perfume that drives women crazy: It smells like money.

—

He was ordered to give up wine, women and song.
"Why don't you get another doctor's opinion?" I asked.
"It wasn't my doctor who told me, it was my accountant!"

—

Two young boys went into a drugstore and bought a box of tampons. The druggist asked if it was for their mother. "Nope," one of the boys said... "But we heard if you used this you could go swimming, horseback riding, and do a lot of other neat things."

—

A young man who's wife was sick charged into the drugstore: "You gave me cyanide instead of Bromide".
"That's terrible!" said the druggist, "You owe me another ten dollars".

~ The Danielle Adams Publishing Company ~

A beautiful blond walked in to a bar in skintight pants with no zipper, no buttons, no closure of any kind, and no apparent way of get them on or off. After staring a while, the man sitting next to her asked "I've been wondering - how do you get into those pants?" She smiled back, "You start by ordering me a drink."

—

I went into a bar the other day, asked for something tall, cold, and full of gin, and the bartender brought out his wife.

—

Fresh from his shower, a woman stood in front of the mirror complaining to her husband that her breasts were too small. Instead of characteristically telling her it's not so, he uncharacteristically comes up with a suggestion.

"If you want your breasts to grow, then every day take a piece of toilet paper and rub it between them for a few seconds."

Willing to try anything, she fetches a piece of toilet paper and stand in front of the mirror, rubbing it between her breasts. 'How long will this take?' She asked.

"They will grow larger over a period of years," her husband replies.

She stopped. 'Do you really think rubbing a piece of toilet paper between my breasts every day will make my breasts larger over the years?"

"Yes, Ma'am," he says, "Worked for your butt, didn't it?"

—

Pilot to copilot, "When was your last sex experience?
    "1955"
    "So long ago?"
Glancing at his watch, "Well, it's only 21:15 now!"

I gave my wife a new watch for her birthday: waterproof, shockproof, unbreakable, antimagnetic - absolutely nothing could happen to it.   She lost it.

—

HOW TO IMPRESS A WOMAN

Wine her and Dine her,
Call her, Hug her,
Hold her, Surprise her,
Compliment her,
Smile at her,
Laugh with her,
Cry with her.
Cuddle with her,
Shop with her,
Give her jewelry,
Buy her flowers,
Hold her hand,
Write love letters to her. Go to the ends of the
earth and back again for her.

HOW TO IMPRESS A MAN

Show up naked
Bring beer

My girlfriend bought a backless, frontless, bottomless, topless evening gown. We just found out it's a belt.

—

A man was sitting in the park when he saw two hearses coming down the block. Behind them was a short man, a Doberman, and a steady procession of men about three blocks long. The man sitting was curious, so he asked the short man what the lengthy procession was about.

"The first hearse is carrying my wife, the second my mother in law. "

The man, his curiosity aroused, asked what happened.

"My dog killed them." Answered the short man. The guy looked down at the dog, then back at the dude, and asked

"Can I borrow him?:"

Pointing over his shoulder the short man replied, "Get in line!"

When a man has a birthday he takes a day off, when a woman has a birthday she takes a year off.

—

What's the difference between an epileptic oyster shucker and a whore with diarrhea? One shucks between fits!

—

The difference between a pickpocket and a peeping tom? A pickpocket snatches watches.

—

What's the difference between a town of tribal pygmies and a girl's track team? Ones a bunch of cunning runts...

—

She went to have her face lifted, but when she found out how much it cost she let the whole thing drop.

There are over ten thousand young women studying law in this country. I think they probably all hope to become mother's in law.

—

Definition of confusion:
20 blind lesbians in a fish market.

—

A man came into the doctor for his review. "I have some good news and some bad news," said the doc. "The bad news is you're gonna' die in about a month." The man fell back, and after several moments caught his breath. "What's the good news?" he asked. "See that beautiful receptionist over there." said the doc... "I'm fucking her!"

—

"I noticed your daughter didn't get home 'til two this morning, while my daughter was in by midnight."
"I know, but you see, my daughter walked home!"

"There's a man across the court taking a shower with the blinds up" complained an old maid at the hotel. The manager dispatched the house detective who came up, looked out the window and said "I can't see a man over there." "Well," said the old woman, "Get up on that table and look again."

—

Complaining that his wife was always away shopping in New York City, he asked his secretary what she would do if she was in his place. "Let's go over to your place" she said, "and I'll show you."

—

A gynecologist was about to examine a patient whose vagina was extremely large. As the doctor approached the table the woman stretched her legs wide apart. Seeing the large cavity he said, "You needn't open so wide, ma'am, you needn't open so wide, ma'am." The patient understanding him the first time, said there was no need to repeat himself. "I didn't," said the doc, "That was an echo."

A man sat next to a young woman with extremely large breasts on an airplane. Unable to break his attention away, he finally asked her if she would - for $ 500.00 - let him kiss them. Needing the money, she consented, and they went to the lavatory where he started nuzzling them. After about ten minutes the lady started to get annoyed, and asked the man if he was going to kiss them. "I'd love to," he said, "But I can't afford it."

—

Eventually she found the macho man of her dreams, but when he took his pants down she noticed he had a two inch cock. "Who do you plan to satisfy with that thing?" She asked. He smiled and promptly replied, "Me!"

—

The small boy watched unimpressed. His father raced back and forth across the lawn towing a spinning kite. No matter how hard he tried, the kite refused to climb. His wife stood on the porch watching. Finally she felt compelled to yell. "Ralph, you need more tail!" The man dropped the kite in disgust. "That's just like a woman," he mumbled. "Last night she told me to go fly a kite!"

—

I'm not going to say his new girl friend is homely, but she sure can catch a Frisbee in her mouth.

—

"What's the difference between fruit salad and a blow job," asked the boss to his secretary? "I don't know." she sighed. "Well then," he replied, "Let's go to lunch."

—

Did you hear about the blind gynecologist who could read lips.

—

A man came into a bar with a rabbit
he said could eat pussy. After a heated
discussion of disbelief, a beautiful woman
took them both back to her apartment, and
showed her crotch to the rabbit - who just sat
there staring. " O.K." Said the man, "Rabbit,
I'm gonna' show you this just one more time".

—

"Hey Mister", said the old hag, "if you've
got twenty bucks, I've got the time."
"No thanks - I've already got a watch!"

—

What's blue and comes in brownies? Cub
Scouts

—

A woman walks into a bar with a duck. A
drunk sitting close by says, "That   is a really
ugly pig you have there."
"It's a duck," says the woman.
"I was talking to the duck!"

—

Last week I invited a beautiful young woman up to my house to see my etchings. She was surprised to get here and not see any etchings, and no furniture at all. In fact, she was floored.

—

She was only the bookkeepers daughter, but she'd let anyone make an entry.

—

There was a country old maid always waiting by the yard, but never getting any male in her box.

—

In the courtroom it takes twelve men to find out if a woman is innocent. On a country road, only one.

—

There was a biologist who crossed an intersection with a convertible and got a blond.

—

Three women applied for the position of secretary. One could spell but not type, one could type but was bad on the phone, and the third was a good typist but couldn't spell. Who got the job? The one with the biggest tits!

—

The rating system in movies today is based on girls. In G movies, no one get the girl. In PG movies, the good guy gets the girl. In R movies, the bad guy gets the girl. In X movies, everyone gets the girl.

—

A man announced aloud in a bar "I'll give 5,000 dollars to any woman who will come back to my house, and meet my terms. A beautiful gamey blonde took him up on his offer. On arrival, he announced they would get naked and have sex for 6 hours straight!. "Are those your terms?" she asked. "Yes... and credit."

—

A man asked a waiter to take a bottle of Merlot to an unusually attractive woman sitting alone at a table in a cozy little restaurant. So the waiter took the Merlot to the woman and said, 'This is from the gentleman who is seated over there,' and indicated the sender with a nod of his head.

She stared at the wine coolly for a few seconds, not looking at the man, then decided to send a reply to him by a note. The waiter, who was lingering nearby for a response, took the note from her and conveyed it to the gentleman.

The note read: 'For me to accept this bottle, you need to have a Mercedes in your garage, a million dollars in the bank and '7' inches in your pants.'

After reading the note, the man decided to compose one of his own in return. He folded the note, handed it to the waiter and instructed him to deliver it to the lady.

It read: 'Just to let you know things aren't always what they appear to be: I have a Ferrari Maranello, BMW Z8, Mercedes CL600, and a Porsche Turbo in my several garages; I have beautiful homes in Aspen, Miami and Hawaii, and a 10,000 acre ranch in Louisiana . There is over twenty million dollars in my bank account and portfolio. But, not even for a woman as beautiful as you, would I cut three inches of my cock. Just send the wine back....'

—

A group of girlfriends is on vacation when they see a 5-story hotel with a sign that reads: "For Women Only". Since they are without their boyfriends and husbands, they decide to go in.

The Bouncer, a very attractive guy, explains to them and once you find what you are looking for, you can stay there. It's easy to decide since each floor has a sign telling you what's inside."

So they start going up and on the first floor the sign reads: "All the men here have it short and thin." The friends laugh and without hesitation move on to the next floor.

The sign on the second floor reads: "All the men here have it long and thin." Still, this isn't good enough so the friends continue on up.

They reach the third floor and the sign reads: "All the men here have it short and thick."

They still want to do better, and so, knowing there are still two floors left, they continued on up.

On the fourth floor, the sign is perfect: "All the men here have it long and thick." The women get all excited and are going in when they realize that there is still one floor left.

Wondering what they are missing, they head on up to the fifth floor. There they find a sign that reads: "There are no men here. This floor was built only to prove that there is no way to please a woman."

———

A beautiful women once said to me, "Give me 8 inches and make it hurt," so I fucked her twice and punched her in the stomach.

—

One day, God was looking down at Earth and saw all of the evil that was going on. He decided to send an angel down to Earth to check it out.

So, He called one of his best angels and sent the angel to Earth for a time.

When she returned she told God, yes it is bad on Earth, 95% is bad and 5% is good. Well, He thought for a moment and said maybe I had better send down a second angel to get another point of view.

So, He called another angel and sent her to Earth for a time too.

When the angel returned she went to Him and told Him, yes, the Earth was in decline, 95% was bad and 5% was good. He said this was not good.

So, He decided to E-mail the 5% that were good as He wanted to encourage them and give them a little something to help keep them going.

Do you know what the E-mail said?

So… You didn't get one either, huh?

A young family moved into a house next to a vacant lot.

One day a construction crew turned up to start building a house on the empty lot. The young family's 6 year old daughter naturally took an interest in all the activity going on next door and started talking with the workers.

She hung around and eventually the construction crew - gems in the rough all of them - more or less adopted her as a kind of project mascot.

They chatted with her, let her sit with them while they had coffee and lunch breaks, and gave her little jobs to do here and there to make her feel important. At the end of the first week they even presented her with a pay envelope containing a dollar.

The little girl took this home to her mother who said all the appropriate words of admiration and suggested that they take the dollar pay she had received to the bank the next day to start a savings account. When they got to the bank the teller was equally impressed with the story and asked the little girl how she had come by her very own pay check at such young age.

The little girl proudly replied, "I've been

working with a crew building a house all week." "My goodness gracious," said the teller, "and will you be working on the house again this week, too"?

"I will if those useless cocksuckers at the lumber yard ever bring us the fucking wood," replied the little girl.

—

When I was 14, I hoped that one day I would have a girlfriend who had big tits.

When I was 16, I got a girlfriend who had large breasts, but there was no passion.

So I decided I needed a passionate girl - with a zest for life. In college I dated a passionate girl, but she was too emotional. Everything was an emergency; she was a drama queen, cried all the time and threatened suicide.

So I decided I needed a girl with stability.

When I was 25 I found a very stable girl but she was boring. She was totally predictable and never got excited about anything. Life became so dull that I decided that I needed a girl with some excitement.

When I was 28 I found an exciting girl, but I couldn't keep up with her. She rushed from one thing to another, never settling on anything. She did mad impetuous things and made me miserable as often as happy. She was great fun initially and very energetic, but directionless.

So I decided to find a girl with some real ambition. When I turned 31, I found a smart ambitious girl with her feet planted firmly on the ground and married her. She was so ambitious that she divorced me and took everything I owned.

Now I'm 57, and am looking for a girl with big tits.

———

The woman's husband had been slipping in and out of a coma for several months, yet she had stayed by his bedside every single day. One day, when he came to, he motioned for her to come nearer.

As she sat by him, he whispered, eyes full of tears, "My dearest, you have been with me all through the bad times. When I got fired, you were there to support me. When my business failed, you were there. When I got shot, you were by my side. When we lost the house, you stayed right here. When my health started failing, you were still by my side. You know what?"

"What dear?" she gently asked, smiling as her heart began to fill with warmth.

"I think you're bad luck."

Men's Issues

IMPORTANT MESSAGE TO WOMEN:

If you think you're fat, you probably are. Don't ask us unless you want the truth. We reserve the right to refuse to answer.

Learn to work the toilet seat. If it's up, put it down.

If you won't dress like the Victoria's Secret girls, don't expect us to act like soap opera guys.

Don't cut your hair. Ever. Long hair is always more attractive than short hair. One of the big reasons guys fear getting married is that married women always cut their hair, and by then you're stuck with her.

Birthdays, Valentines, and Anniversaries are not quests to see if we can find the perfect present yet again!

If you ask a question you don't want an honest answer to, expect an answer you don't want to hear.

Sometimes, we're not thinking about you. Accept it. Don't ask us what we're thinking about unless you are prepared to discuss such topics as navel lint, the shotgun formation, or monster trucks.

Sunday = sports. It's like the full moon or the changing of the tides.

Shopping is not a sport, and no, we're never going to think of it that way.

When we have to go somewhere, absolutely anything you wear is fine. Really.

You have enough clothes.

You have too many shoes.

Crying is blackmail.

Ask for what you want. Let's be clear: Subtle hints don't work. Strong hints don't work. Really obvious hints don't work. Just say it!

No, we don't know what day it is. We never will. Please mark anniversaries on the calendar.

~ The Danielle Adams Publishing Company ~

Peeing standing up is more difficult. We're bound to miss sometimes.

Most guys own three pairs of shoes. What makes you think we'd be any good at choosing which pair, out of thirty, would look good with your dress?

"Yes" and "No" are perfectly acceptable answers to almost every question.

Come to us with a problem only if you want help solving it. That's what we do. Sympathy is what your girlfriends are for.

A headache that lasts for 17 months is a problem. See a doctor.

Foreign films are best left to foreigners.

It is neither in your best interest nor ours to take the quiz together. No, it doesn't matter which quiz.

Anything we said 6 months ago is inadmissible in an argument. All comments become null and void after 7 days.

If something we said can be interpreted two ways, and one of the ways makes you sad or angry, we meant the other one.

Let us ogle. We're going to look anyway; it's genetic.

You can either tell us to do something OR tell us how to do something, but not both.

Whenever possible, please say whatever you have to say during commercials.

ALL men see in only 16 colors. Peach is a fruit, not a color.

If it itches, we scratch it.

Snack foods are as exciting for us as handbags are for you.

If we ask what's wrong and you say "nothing," we will act like nothing's wrong. We know you're lying, but it's just not worth the hassle.

Men are driven by two things - sex and hunger. If we just had sex, please make me a sandwich.

Blonds

Two blondes were going to Disneyland. They were driving on the Interstate when they saw the sign that said Disneyland LEFT. They started crying and turned around and went home.

FLORIDA OR MOON

Two blondes living in Oklahoma were sitting on a bench talking, and one blonde says to the other, 'Which do you think is farther away... Florida or the moon?'

The other blonde turns and says 'Hellooooooooooo, can you see Florida ?????'

CAR TROUBLE

A blonde pushes her BMW into a gas station. She tells the mechanic it died. After he works on it for a few minutes, it is idling smoothly.

She says, 'What's the story?'

He replies, 'Just crap in the carburetor.'

She asks, 'How often do I have to do that?'

SPEEDING TICKET

A police officer stops a blonde for speeding and asks her very nicely if he could see her licence.

She replied in a huff, 'I wish you guys would get your act together. Just yesterday you take away my license and then today you ask me to show it to you!'

RIVER WALK

There's this blonde out for a walk. She comes to a river and sees another blonde on the opposite bank 'Yoo-hoo!' she shouts, 'How can I get to the other side?'

The second blonde looks up the river then down the river and shouts back, 'You ARE on the other side.'

AT THE DOCTOR'S OFFICE

A gorgeous young redhead goes into the doctor's office and said that her body hurt wherever she touched it.
'Impossible!' says the doctor.. 'Show me.'

The redhead took her finger, pushed on her left shoulder and screamed, then she pushed her elbow and screamed even more. She pushed her knee and screamed; likewise she pushed her ankle and screamed. Everywhere she touched made her scream.

The doctor said,
'You're not really a redhead, are you?
'Well, no' she said, 'I'm actually a blonde.'
'I thought so,' the doctor said, 'Your finger is broken.'

KNITTING

A highway patrolman pulled alongside a speeding car on the freeway. Glancing at the car, he was astounded to see that the blonde behind the wheel was knitting!

Realizing that she was oblivious to his flashing lights and siren, the trooper cranked down his window, turned on his bullhorn and yelled, 'PULL OVER!'

'NO!' the blonde yelled back, 'IT'S A SCARF!'

BLONDE ON THE SUN

A Russian, an American, and a Blonde were talking one day.

The Russian said, 'We were the first in space!'

The American said, 'We were the first on the moon!'

The Blonde said, 'So what? We're going to be the first on the sun!' The Russian and the American looked at each other and shook their heads.

'You can't land on the sun, you idiot! You'll burn up!' said the Russian.

To which the Blonde replied, 'We're not stupid, you know. We're going at night!'

IN A VACUUM

A blonde was playing Trivial Pursuit one night...

It was her turn. She rolled the dice and she landed on Science & Nature. Her question was, 'If you're in a vacuum and someone calls your name, can you hear it?'

She thought for a time and then asked, 'Is it on or off?'

FINALLY

A girl was visiting her blonde friend, who had acquired two new dogs, and asked her what their names were.

The blonde responded by saying that one was named Rolex and one was named Timex..

Her friend said, 'Whoever heard of someone naming dogs like that?'

'HELLLOOOOOOO......,' answered the blonde. 'They're watch dogs'!

"Did you hear my last joke?"
"I sure hope so!"

Overheard...

"Carry your bag sir?"
"No, let her walk!"

"Is your sister spoiled?
"No, that's just her perfume!"

"Does your wife like housework?"
"She likes nothing better!"

"My girl has a great personality!"
"Mine isn't good looking either."

"Sir, did the mud pack help your wife's appearance?"
"It did for a few days, but then it fell off."

"Here is a picture of my wife."
"She must be very wealthy."

"My wife ran away with another man
in my new car!"
"Good God! Not in your new car!"

"But how can I be overdrawn, I still
have 25 checks left?"

"Does your wife pick your clothes?"
"No, just the pockets."

"I've been cooking for you for ten years!"
"You ought to be done by now."

"You don't need to open your mouth
that far madam, I expect to be standing
outside when I pull your tooth."

"I'm going to get a divorce. My wife
hasn't spoken to me in 6 months."
"Better think it over - wives like that are
hard to find."

"Madam, have your eyes ever been checked?"
"No, doctor - they've always been
brown."

"I had the same old thing for breakfast
with my wife this morning: an argument!"

"If your wife were driving in the car
ahead of you, and stuck her hand out of the
window, and gestured toward the approaching
corner, what would it mean?"
        "It would mean the window's open"

"May I take you home, honey?"
        "Sure, where do you live?"

"My wife gave me steak three times last week,
        and steak three times this week."
"So your new wife is a great cook?"
        "No, it was the same steak."

"Is your wife outspoken?"
        "Not by anyone I know of."

"Do you believe in clubs for women?"
        "Only when everything else fails."

"Say when."
        "After this drink!"

Father: "How old would a person be who was
born is 1920?"
Son: "Man or woman?"

"My wife obeys me perfectly!"
"Amazing! How do you do it?"
"I tell her to do as she pleases."

"You unattached?"
"No, just put together sloppily."

Husband to wife who's driving:
"I don't know where you're going to park -
- I don't see any empty blocks."

"Did you sleep with my wife?"
"Not a wink"

"How do you look when I'm sober?"

"Who was that pretty blond I saw you outwit
last night?"

"Am I the first girl you ever kissed?"
"Quite possibly - were you in Atlantic
city in 1995?"

"How many drinks does it take to make you dizzy?"

"Three, and don't call me dizzy."

"Of course I've kissed girls before - you didn't think I'd use you as a guinea pig, did you?"

"Sir, I'm afraid your wife has V.D."

"Could she have caught it in a public rest room?"

"It's possible, but it certainly would have been uncomfortable."

One cannibal to another: "Your wife sure makes good soup."

"Yea, but I'm gonna' miss her!"

Tarzan, on meeting Jane: "What name?"

"Jane."

"What whole name?"

"Vagina."

"Floors please." said the elevator operator.

"Ballroom!" Said the gentlemen in the back.

"Oh. Sorry!" said the young lady, "I didn't realize I was crowding you.

"John, you've been to the bar 6 times already"
    "It's OK dear - I've been telling everyone
I'm getting them for you."

Wife: "I've changed my mind"
    Husband: "Does it work better, now?"

"How'd you make out in that fight with your
wife last night?"
"She came crawling to me on hands and
knees."
"Yeah? What'd she say?"
"Come out from under the bed, you coward!"

    "Am I tired - I've been running around
here all day trying to get something for my
wife."
    "Have any offers yet?"

"I'm telling you for the last time to get your
hand off my breast."
    "Ha! I knew you'd weaken!"

"Before we were married you told me you
were well off!"
    "I was, but I didn't know it!"

~ The Danielle Adams Publishing Company ~

"Has your wife changed much since you've been married?"

"Yes - she's changed my habits and my friends."

"When is your sister thinking of getting married?"

"Constantly."

"How long did you work for your husband?"

"Until I got him."

"Say you love me!"

"You love me!"

"My wife took everything and left me!"

"You're lucky, mine didn't leave!"

"Pardon me lady, but I'm writing a telephone book. May I have your number."

"What was your biggest vacation expense?"

"My wife."

"Whom are you working for?"

"Same people. My wife and four kids."

"I can make my wife do anything
she want's to do!

I have a lovely wife. And It's not just my
opinion... it's her's.

Husband to wife when he came home late:
"You look like I need a drink.

"What does a woman put behind her ears
to make herself more attractive?"
Dr. Mann: "Her feet."

Ask Dr. Mann

Questions with Dr. Mann:

What kind of man do you look up to?
Dr. Mann, "I admire a man who not only
knows how to hold a girl tight, but knows how
to get her that way."

Dr., can you tell me what you do when a girl
faints?
Dr. Mann: "I stop kissing her."

"How many men does it take to mop a floor?"
Dr. Mann: "None. It's a woman's job".

"Do you think women have more to say than
men?"
Dr. Mann: "No, they merely use more
words."

"How do you tell when a woman is having an
orgasm?"
Dr. Mann: "Who cares."

"Why Do Women Get Cramps?"
Dr. Mann: "They deserve them!"

Why did God invent women?
Dr. Mann: "Because sheep can't type."

"Do men live longer than their wives?"
"Dr. Mann: "No. It merely seems longer."

"How can you tell how old a woman is?"
Dr. Mann: "By counting the rings under her eyes.

"Why don't most companies give women more than a half an hour off for lunch?"
Dr. Mann: "They don't want to have to retrain them."

"Why are women like clams?"
Dr. Mann: "When the red tide comes, you don't eat them."

"Why do women have pussies?"
Dr. Mann: "So men will talk to them."

"Why did God invent liquor?"

Dr. Mann: "So fat ugly girls could get laid, too."

"How can you tell who the head nurse in a hospital is?"

Dr. Mann: "By the dirt on her knees."

"How can I cure my wife of bed wetting?"

Dr. Mann: "Give her an electric blanket."

"Why Do women have two holes?"

Dr. Mann: "So when they get drunk you can carry them home like a six-pack."

"How do you fuck a fat woman?"

Dr. Mann: "Roll her in flour and go for the wet spot!"

"Why don't they let girls swim in the ocean any more?"

Dr. Mann: "They can't get the smell out of the fish."

"Dr. Mann, how do you as a physician feel about masturbating?"

Dr. Mann: "If you masturbate, you only do it when you're in the mood, you always know who you're dealing with, you know when you've had enough, and you don't have to be polite to someone cranky afterwards." Sex is like bridge - when you have a good hand you don't especially need a partner.

"What is the difference between a foxy woman and an ugly broad?"

Dr. Mann: "About 9 drinks."

"Why isn't a man allowed to have more than one wife?"

Dr. Mann: "The law protects those who are not able to protect themselves.

"What do you do if a woman gives you the slip?"

Dr. Mann: "Try to get the panties, too."

"Doctor, does it take longer for older women to climax?"

Dr. Mann: "Who cares."

"Is anything better than a 69?"

Dr. Mann: "Yes, a 68 - she does you and you owe her one."

"What's the best thing about women's lib?"

Dr. Mann: "It gives the girls something to do in their spare time."

"Why do women get married?"

Dr. Mann: "To have someone to spend with the rest of their life."

"My wife complains she gave me the best years of her life!"

Dr. Mann: "Ask her who made them her best years."

"What do lesbians do for dinner?"

Dr. Mann: "Eat out."

"Do you believe God made woman in Her Image?"

Doctor Mann: "If She did, why didn't She make her so that she could take a piss standing up?"

"Really, why are there women?"
    Dr. Mann: "Because sheep can't cook."

"Why do doctors think women are descended
from mermaids?"
    Dr. Mann: "Because they smell like fish
below the waist."

"Tell us about yourself."
    Dr. Mann: "I like to think of myself as a
man who comes and goes."

"Ever have an interesting case late at night?"
    Dr. Mann: "A man called me at 3 AM
and said: "Doc, come right over, my wife
swallowed a corkscrew." As the I was putting
on my coat, a second call came in - "It's OK,
Doc, we found another one."

"What can you give to a woman who has
everything?"
    Dr. Mann: "My phone number."

"You seem to be very harsh on women - even
you have to admit there are beautiful and

refined girls who you appreciate."

Dr. Mann: "Refined girls are nothing more than cheap girls who have learned to keep their elbows off the table."

"Doctor, what do most women look for in a husband?"

Dr. Mann: "Appearance - usually the sooner the better."

"What is the best way for a woman to preserve her wedding ring?"

Dr. Mann: "Dip it in dishwater three times a day."

"Is it unlucky to postpone a wedding?"

Dr. Mann: "No, not if you keep postponing it!"

"Someone told me you don't fool around with women?"

Dr. Mann: "That's not true. What I said was when it comes to women, I don't fool around."

"Piss."

Men Words

Men Words, men's sayings: some women don't like to use certain words - and in fact, some of these words really piss women off. And the sayings can only be heard out of the mouths of men. Manly men.

If you're not doing anything tonight, why don't you copy these words down, and send them to Hilary Clinton. Ever notice some women just can't take a joke. See how many of these words you can use in a sentence.

Bitch.
Twat!
Piss.
Takin' a piss!
It's hard and I'm ready.
Fuck 'em.
Don't worry, I'll pull out in time.
I've never met a woman like you.
I'll only put it in a little.
I won't come in your mouth.
Show me your tits!

Q: Why is a fat girl like a moped?
   A: They're both fun to ride till a friend sees you.

Burning Questions About Women

Q: What did the blind man say when he passed the fish market?
   A: "Good Morning Ladies!"

Q: What do fat women do in the summer?
   A: Stick!

Q: What's the main difference between your job and your wife?
   A: After five years your job still sucks.

Q: What's the difference between parsley and pussy?
   A: Nobody eats parsley.

Q: What is the first thing a sorority girl does in the morning?
   A: Walks home.

Q: Are sheep better than women for sex?
   A: Yes! They're always in the mood.

They never have a headache.

When you're through screwing them you can eat them.

You don't have to polite to some bitch afterwards!"

Q: Why is a woman like an oven?

A: They both need to be heated up before you stick in the meat.

Q: Why are women are like screen doors?

A: They loosen up once they get banged a few times.

Q: Why are women like Jello?

A: They both squirm when you eat them.

Q: Why don't they have real grass in football stadiums in Iowa?

A: So the cheerleaders don't graze at halftime.

Q: Why are women like baseball umpires?

A: They make quick decisions, never reverse them, and they don't think you're safe when you're out.

Q: What's the difference between a donkey, and a blow job?

A: You can beat a donkey, but you can't beat a blow job!

Q: How does a cub scout become a boy scout?

A: He eats a brownie.

Q: How many animals live in a pair of panty hose?

A: Two calves, ten little piggies, one pussy, one ass, a thousand hares, sometimes crabs, and a dead fish nobody can ever find.

Q: What is the difference between a hungry women and a starving dog?

A: If you pick up a starving dog and feed him, he will not bite you.

Q: How can a real man tell if his girlfriend is having an orgasm?

A: Real men don't care.

Q: What's a modern definition of Cinderella?

A: A woman who fucks like crazy and at midnight turns into a pizza and a six-pack.

Q: Why did the American lesbian come back from her visit to Europe early?
A: She missed her native tongue.

Q: What's better than roses on your piano?
A: Two lips on your organ.

Q: Why are women like pianos?
A: When they're not upright, they're grand!

Q: What do you call a prostitute with a runny nose?
A: Full.

Q: What's the difference between a magician and a chorus line.
A: The magician has cunning feats and stunts.

Q: What's better than honor?
A: In'er.

Q: Why is a woman like a roll of toilet paper?
A: Because after you tear off the first piece, the rest comes easily.

Q: What is the biggest problem for an atheist?
A: No one to talk to during orgasm.

Q. What do you call a smart blonde?
A: A golden retriever.

Q: Why does the bride always wear white?
A: Because it is good for the dishwasher to match the stove and refrigerator.

Q: What is the difference between a battery and a woman?
A: A battery has a positive side.

Q: A brunette, a blonde, and a redhead are all in fifth grade. Who has the biggest tits?
A: The blonde, because she should be in tenth grade.

Q: What's the difference between a terrorist and a Jewish mother?
A: You can negotiate with the terrorist!

Q: Do you know the punishment for bigamy?
A: Two mothers-in-law!

If your wife want's to learn how to drive, don't stand in her way.

Wives... and other strange stories

My wife's the most wonderful girl in the world - and that's not just my opinion - it's hers!

My secretary reminds me of my wife... every time I whisper softly in her ear she says "Remember, you have a wife!"

If you want your wife to listen, talk to another woman.

I wish I could afford another wife. I really don't want another wife, I could just use the money.

I know a man who got a bottle of cognac for his wife - it was a wonderful exchange.

A good wife is one who thinks twice before saying nothing.

When it comes to housework, most wives likes to do nothing better.

A wife is someone who will tie a string around your finger to remind you to mail a letter, then forget to give it to you. Then blame you for not mailing it.

For twenty years my wife and I were very happy - then we met.

Whenever I meet a woman who would make a good wife, she is.

My wife's got everything - and I wish I could get some of it back.

I'd like to smother my wife in diamonds but there must be a cheaper way.

I wouldn't say my wife is smart, but her I.Q. is 20:20.

My wife and I exchanged gifts - I gave her a beaver coat, and she exchanged it for a mink coat.

Incompatibility: you give your wife a gift certificate, and she exchanges it.

Several years ago I asked for her hand and it's been in my pocket ever since.

Even my accountant can't figure his wife out!

A wife laughs at her husbands jokes not because they are clever but because she is.

If you want to see a baseball game in the worst way, take your wife.

I was trying to get a new car for my wife, but nobody would swap.

You think you've got it tough - every time my wife sees a parking space she begs me to buy her a new car.

The garbage man came early yesterday, my wife went running out with a small sack yelling "Am I too late?" "No!" said the driver, "Jump in."

For Christmas my wife told me all she wants is a five pound box of money.

If your wife becomes fat, tell her to go to a paint store and get thinner.

Am I happily married? I'll bet you don't have a wife who worships and adores you. Well, neither do I.

I brought my wife to the convention. It was a question of bringing her along, or kissing her goodbye.

Unlike most brides my wife can boil water, but I get tired of boiled water seven times a week.

You know you're getting old when you don't care where your wife goes, just so you don't have to go along with her.

The honeymoon is over when your dog brings you your slippers and your wife barks at you.

A wife is someone who loves her husband for all he's worth.

A woman marries a man expecting he will change, but he doesn't. A man marries a woman expecting that she won't change, but she does.

A woman worries about the future until she gets a husband.
A man never worries about the future until he gets a wife.

A married man should forget his mistakes. There's no use in two people remembering the same thing!

Without his wife he wouldn't be what he is today - broke.

Nothing makes a little knowledge so dangerous as thinking your wife doesn't have it.

The man who thought up a $600 tax deduction for your wife must have been a bachelor.

When a man opens the door of his car for his wife you can be sure that either the car or the wife is new.

A little honey is good for your health, unless your wife finds out.

I've had bad luck with both my wives - the first one divorced me, and the second one won't.

My wife must be home, the phone is still warm.

Wife: An attachment you screw on the bed to get the housework done.

DEFINITIONS

Diamonds -
One of the hardest substances known to man - especially to get back

Flowers -
A gift brought by men to accompany a weak alibi.

Imagination -
Something that sits up with a wife when her husband is out.

Alimony -
A contraction of 'All His Money'

Bachelor -
A happy go lucky fellow who believes in wine, women, and so-long.

Bigamist -
> — A man who makes the same mistake twice.
> — A man who loves not wisely but two well.
> — A man who has married an attractive woman and a good cook.
> — An individual who keeps two himself.

Two Bagger -
A woman who is so ugly you not only put a bag on her head, but you put a bag on your head in case her bag breaks.

Marriage -
A process where love ripens into vengeance.

Courting -
Future tense of the word "Caught."

Executive -
One who if given enough rope gets tied up at the office with his secretary.

Gentlemen -
— One who never beats his wife without provocation.
— A man who when his wife drops something, kicks it over to where she can pick it up more easily.
— A man who opens the door when his wife is carrying two bags of groceries.

Womanhood -
One of the louder figures of speech.

Lawyer -
A man who would stay up all night trying be break a woman's will.

Intuition -
— A unique instinct that tells a woman she's right, whether she is or not.
— A sixth sense that allows a woman 5 wrong guesses.

Second Story Man -
One who is always ready with a second story if his wife doesn't believe his first one.

Mink Coat -
Something you give your wife to keep her warm, or quiet.

Monogamy -
Same as bigamy: having one wife too many.

Bitch -
One who complains about the noise he makes when her husband fixes his own breakfast.

Woman -
Life support system for a pussy.

Wedding -
A ceremony at which a man loses control of himself.

Wedding ring -
— The world's smallest handcuff.
— A tourniquet that stops a man's circulation.

Youthful Figure -
    What you get when you ask a woman her age.

Love -
    — The delusion that one woman differs from another.
    — A passion, which makes time pass, as distinguished from marriage - which makes love pass.

Beauty contest -
    A show where they judge young ladies on looks, talent, and poise... then crown the one with the biggest tits.

Adolescence -
    When a girl's voice changes from no to yes.

Alimony -
    That which enables a woman who at one time lived happily married to live happily unmarried.

Bride -
  A woman who puts her foot down as soon as her husband has carried her over the threshold.

Wedding cake -
  A cake which once eaten, gives you indigestion the rest of your life.

Coyote ugly -
  When you wake up besides a woman that is so ugly, rather than pulling your arm out from under her head and chance waking her, you gnaw off your arm and leave.

Husband -
One who never knows when he's well off - because he never is.

Why It's GREAT To Be A Guy!!!!

* Your ass is never a factor in a job interview.
* Your orgasms are real. Always.
* Your last name stays put.
* The garage is all yours.
* Nobody secretly wonders if you swallow.
* Wedding plans take care of themselves.
* You don't have to curl up next to a hairy ass every night.
* Chocolate is just another snack.
* You can be President.
* You can wear a white shirt to a water park.
* Foreplay is optional.
* You never feel compelled to stop a friend from getting laid.
* Car mechanics tell you the truth.
* You don't give a rat's ass if someone notices your new haircut.
* Hot wax never comes near your genitals.
* You never have to drive to another gas station because this one's "just too icky."
* Same work... more pay.
* Wrinkles add character.
* You don't have to leave the room to make emergency crotch adjustments.

* Wedding Dress $2000; Tux rental $100.
* $1.50 a shirt dry cleaning.
* If you retain water, it's in a canteen.
* People never glance at your chest when you are talking to them.
* Princess Di's death was just another obituary.
* The occasional well-rendered belch is practically expected.
* New shoes don't cut, blister, or mangle your feet.
* Porn movies are designed with you in mind.
* Not liking a person does not preclude having great sex with them.
* Your pals can be trusted never to trap you with: "So, notice anything different?"
* One mood, all the time.
* And the world is your urinal, because you can take a piss just about anywhere.

A Good Woman Will Always Say...

> "You know, I've been complaining a lot lately. I don't blame you for ignoring me."

> "I know it's late and my parents are in the other room... but I still want you right now!"

> "This porno storyline is boring... Fast forward to the gang bang scenes."

> "Don't move over, I kind'a like sleeping in the wet spot."

> "Don't dirty up your good T-shirt wiping that up. Here, use my blouse."

> "That was a lot of fun! When will all of your friends be over again to watch pornos?"

> "I bet it would be kinky to watch you with our French maid, Monique."

> "You're my daddy! Oh, yes, you're my daddy!"

> "The new girl in my office used to be a stripper. I invited her over for dinner on Friday."
>
> "Honey, you forgot to flush the toilet. But it's good to see your so regular!"

> "While you were in the bathroom, they went for it on fourth down and missed. If they can hold them to a field goal they'll still cover."

> "Bar food again!? Fabulous!"

> "I liked that wedding even more than ours. Your ex-girlfriend has real style."
>
> "That girl is wearing the same outfit as I am. Cool! I'm gonna go over and compliment her."
>
> "I love hearing those cute stories about your old girlfriends. Please tell me more."
>
> "I like using this new lawn mower so much more than the old one, what a wonderful Valentines Day present. Thanks."

> "Let's just leave the toilet seat up at all times. That way you don't have to mess with it anymore."

> "I've decided to get myself a boob job. How big do you want 'em?"

> "It's only the third quarter, you should order a couple more pitchers."

> "Honey come here! Watch me do a tequila shot off of Stephanie's bare ass!"

> "I'll just put it on my credit card, so order another round for you and your friends."

> "I'm so happy with my new hairstyle, I don't think I'll ever change it again."

> "Damn! I love when my pillow smells so manly - like your cigars, scotch and morning breath. You passed out again before brushing your teeth, didn't you?"

> "You are so much smarter than my father!"

> "If we're not going to have sex, then you have to let me watch the football game!"

> "I know you may not feel like sex right now, but at least let me give you a blow job..."

They seem to be the perfect couple - she waxes the floors, and he takes a bottle and polishes it off.

Marriage

I never knew happiness till I got married - then it was too late.

Some women don't marry a man for his money, but they sure seem to divorce him for it.

Alimony is the system whereby two people make a mistake and one continues to pay for it.

Anyone who thinks marriage is a 50/50 proposition doesn't know the half of it.

If you think it's a 50/50 proposition, you don't know fractions.

Marriage: A very expensive way to get your laundry done free.

Marriage is like a cafeteria - you pick something out that looks good and you pay later.

Marriage - the word that is a sentence.

Marriage is an educational institution in which a man loses his bachelor's degree, and a woman gets her master's.

I'm going down to city hall to see if my marriage license has expired. I keep reading it for loopholes!

Every time I meet a beautiful girl either she is married or I am.

Remember: When women file for divorce they all ask for custody of the money.

I only know of two kinds of women: those who want to get married, and those who haven't the slightest desire not to.

If weddings are such happy occasions why does the groom wear black?

Some women are remarkable housekeepers - they get a divorce and they keep the house.

She's sticking to him through all the trouble he never would have had if he hadn't married her in the first place.

The first year is the paper anniversary. After one year you're beaten to a pulp.

Marriage is like eating in a restaurant - After you've ordered, you notice what someone else has, and you wish you had taken that.

Second Marriage - the triumph of hope over experience.

Marriage is like a three ring circus: Engagement ring, wedding ring, suffering.

People wouldn't be getting divorced for such foolish, flimsy reasons if they didn't get married for such foolish, flimsy reasons.

Marriage is an institution that teaches you patience, broad-mindedness, tolerance, and a lot of other things you wouldn't need if you weren't married.

Make love not war. Hell, do both: get married!

Adam: "I'm 88, and getting married next month."
Doc: "And how old is your bride?"
Adam: "22"
Doc: "Sex could be fatal!"
Adam: "Well, if she dies, she dies."

If all brides are beautiful, where do so many ugly housewives come from.

Marriage is a continuous process of getting used to things you don't expect.

She didn't want to marry him for his money, but that was the only way she could get it.

All marriages are happy - it's the living together afterwards that causes all the trouble.

Marrying a woman for her beauty is like buying a house for it's paint.

I shouldn't say too much bad about women, they still make the best wives.

Give a girl enough rope, and she'll ring a wedding bell.

Husbands are like wood fires, left unattended they go out.

Every time a bride gets a shower a groom gets soaked.

Alimony is like paying for a meal after you've lost your appetite.

There are two kinds of wives: those with wealthy husbands, and those who act like they have wealthy husbands.

All wives have the last word - some have it in arguments, some have it in clothes.

Just think - if it weren't for marriage, men would go though life thinking they had no faults at all.

The most effective way to remember your wife's birthday is to forget it once.

"Say waiter, what time is it?"
"Sorry, this isn't my table."

Men Jokes

What did George Washington say before crossing the Delaware?
"Get in the boat, men."

What did the rake say to the hoe?
"Hi, hoe!"

What does a hen do when she stands on one foot?
Lifts up the other one.

Man: "I want this suit in the window."
Storekeeper: "It is in the window!"

What did the termite say when he walked into the bar?
"Is the bar tender here?"

Two guys were walking down the street when they came across a dog in obvious enjoyment licking his dick. "Wow, don't you wish you could do that?" One said. "Naa," came the reply, "The dog would probably bite me."

Q: How do you get a cross eyed girl pregnant?
    A: You fuck her.

Know why girls rub their eyes when they wake up? They don't have balls to scratch.

I get laid almost every night.
    I almost got laid Monday night, I almost got laid Tuesday night...

Know why dogs lick their balls?
    They can.

Upon coming back from a vacation at a nudist camp, a friend said his first three days were the hardest.

Know the difference between meat and fish?
    If you beat your fish it dies.

Q: What has 100 Balls and fucks rabbits?
    A: A Shotgun.

Two men were talking, "I don't see how women can spend so much money - my wife doesn't smoke, doesn't drink, doesn't do drugs, and she has her own pussy."

~ The Danielle Adams Publishing Company ~

"Of course you can buy that hat dear, I like that middle aged look it gives you."

"Of course you can buy that dress dear, my secretary has one just like it!"

"You play golf? What's your handicap?"
"A wife and three kids."

A wife returning from a golf match catches her husband with another woman and bludgeons him with her golf club. The police come and ask what happened. She said "I hit him with a 5 iron." The police asked how many times. "I don't know," said the women tearfully — "4, 5, maybe 6? Just put me down for a 4.

Q: What's red and smells like blue paint?
   A: Red paint.

I was going to ask God for a bike, but I know God doesn't work like that. So I stole a bike and asked for forgiveness.

Knowledge is knowing a tomato is a fruit. Wisdom is knowing not to put it in a fruit salad.

Going to church doesn't make you a Christian any more than standing in a garage makes you a car.

Women will never be equal to men until they can walk down the street with a bald head and a beer gut and still think they're sexy.

America: where you get the choice of two people for president, and 50 for Miss America.

Never hit a man with glasses. Hit him with a baseball bat.

If 4 out of 5 people suffer from diarrhoea, does that mean one enjoys it?

To steal ideas from one person is plagiarism, To steal from many, research.

Remember, it's not "How high are you?" it's "Hi, how are you?"

I just wrote a joke with no punch line...

Why don't women blink during foreplay?
Because they don't have enough time.

More Questions about Men and Women

Why does it take 1 million sperm to fertilize one egg?
They won't stop for directions

Why did god put men on earth?
Because a vibrator can't mow the lawn

Why don't women have men's brains?
Because they don't have penises to put them in

What do electric trains and breasts have in common?
They're intended for children but men usually end up playing with them

Why do men snore when they lie on their backs?
Because their balls fall over their assholes and they vapor lock

Why do men masturbate?
It is sex with someone they love.

Why were men given larger brains than dogs?
So they won't hump women's legs at cocktail parties.

Why is a man's pee yellow and his sperm white?
So he can tell if he's coming or going.

How many men does it take to put a toilet seat down?
Nobody knows.

Why does a woman always have the last word in any argument?
Anything a man says after that is the beginning of a new argument.

Q: What's the difference between a girlfriend and a wife?
A: 45 lbs.

Q: What's the difference between a boyfriend and a husband?
A: 45 minutes.

~ The Danielle Adams Publishing Company ~

Q: What is it when a man talks nasty to a woman?

A: Sexual harassment.

Q: What is it when a woman talks nasty to a man?

A: $3.99 a minute.

Q: How can you tell if your wife is dead?
A: The sex is the same but the dishes pile up.

(Q: How can you tell if your husband is dead?
A: The sex is the same but you get the remote.)

Q: What's it called when a woman is paralyzed from the waist down?

A: Marriage.

Q: If your wife keeps coming out of the kitchen to nag you, what have you done wrong?

A: Made her chain too long.

Q: How many women does it take to change a light bulb?

A: None, they just sit there in the dark and complain.

Q. Why are men and parking spaces alike?
A. Because all the good ones are gone and the only ones left are disabled.

Q. Why is it so hard for women to find men that are sensitive, caring, and good-looking?
A. Because those men already have boyfriends.

Q. What is a man's view of safe sex?
A. A padded headboard.

Q. How do men sort their laundry?
A. "Filthy" and "Filthy but Wearable"

Q. Do you know why women fake orgasm?
A. Because men fake foreplay.

Q. What's the difference between a new wife and a new dog?
A. After a year, the dog is still excited to see you.

Q. What makes men chase women they have no intention of marrying?
A. The same urge that makes dogs chase cars they have no intention of driving.

Q. What is the biggest problem for an atheist?
A. No one to talk to during orgasm.

Q. What do you call a smart blonde?
A. A golden retriever.

Q. What do you call an Amish guy with his hand up a horse's ass?
A. A mechanic!

Q. Who is the most popular guy at the nudist colony?
A. The guy who can carry a cup of coffee in each hand and a dozen donuts.

Q. Who is the most popular girl at the nudist colony?
A. She is the one who can eat the last donut!

Q. Why does the bride always wear white?
A. Because it is good for the dishwasher to match the stove and refrigerator.

Q. What is the difference between a battery and a woman?
A. A battery has a positive side.

Q. A brunette, a blonde, and a redhead are all in seventh grade. Who has the biggest tits?
A. The blonde, because she's 19.

Q. Why don't pygmies wear tampons?
A. They keep stepping on the strings.

Q. Did you hear about the guy who finally figured out women?
A. Neither did I

Q. Do you know the punishment for bigamy?
A. Two mothers-in-law!

Q: Why do hookers make more money than drug dealers?
A: A hooker can clean her crack and sell it again.

Q: What is the definition of "making love"?
A: Something a woman does while a guy is humping her.

Q: What would you call a lesbian with thick fingers?
A: Well-hung.

Q: What's the difference between Hard and Light?

A: Even though its difficult, you can go to sleep with a light on.

Q: What's the difference between erotic and kinky?

A: Erotic is when you use a feather. Kinky is when you use the whole chicken.

Q. What are the small bumps around a woman's nipples for?

A. Its Braille for "suck here."

Q. Why do women have tits?

A. So men will talk to them

Q. Why do women rub their eyes when they get up in the morning?

A. They don't have balls to scratch.

Women Stuff

If it wasn't for women, we wouldn't have this shit:

Doilies
Wallpaper with tiny designs on it
Bells on Cats
Toy Poodles
Fringed Pillows
Mauve & Taupe
(What the hell color is Taupe, anyway!)
Hot Pink
Perfume
Tampons
The balance beam
Puce
Fuzzy slippers
Clear Plastic Slip Covers
Bath Shoppes
Calories
Depilatory
Panties
Eyebrow Pluckers, Fingernail Polish,
Hair Curlers, hot rollers, and False
Eyelashes
And you could take a piss anywhere!

~ The Danielle Adams Publishing Company ~

Automobile Sayings

What good would a manly man book be if it didn't include a chapter on automobiles. Whether you love them or hate them, pretty much all men have a passion for cars.

I don't know too many women who know about cars. I mean women are nice for certain things, but how can you have a serious conversation with someone who doesn't know what a carburetor is - or what a lug wrench is for.

Picture this: You're riding down a dark road. Traffic is light. It's slightly past midnight. The red of a distant stoplight glares off the hood of your car. As you coast to a stop, a beautiful woman suddenly pulls up next to you in an immaculate white Corvette.

You stare at her. She glances in your direction. It's a good thing you waxed your car last month, Ford Falcons are hard to get, especially one in this good a condition. You vacuumed, too.

You know when the light changes you know you may never see her again. What do you do? Hold up these pages.

Seriously, this book is designed to be a companion to you in your car. When you see a nice looking lady in the car next to you, hold any of the following pages up to the window. You never know, you could get lucky. Have a good time!

~ The Danielle Adams Publishing Company ~

Show me your tits!

OK - Just Show Me One Tit!

I can make you happy with my tongue!

I'm hung like a loaf of Italian Bread.

My
other car
is a
Ford
Fairlane!

I can lick my eye-brows!

Of course I'm drunk! What do you think I am, a stunt driver?

If you don't like the way I'm driving, you come get these handcuffs off!

~ The Danielle Adams Publishing Company ~

Next Time, Wave ALL your fingers at me!

Just Blink if you want SEX.

~ The Danielle Adams Publishing Company ~

103 More Reasons it's Great to be a Guy

1. Phone conversations are over in 30 seconds flat.
2. Movie nudity is virtually always female.
3. You know stuff about military hardware.
4. A week's holiday requires only one suitcase.
5. 99% of the XBox games were made for you.
6. You don't have to monitor your friends' sex lives.
7. Queues for the toilet are 90% shorter.
8. You can open all your own jars.
9. Old friends don't bitch about you if you've lost or gained weight.
10. Dry cleaners and haircutter's don't rob you blind.
11. When channel surfing, you don't have to stall on every shot of someone crying.
12. Your ass is never a factor in a job interview.
13. All your orgasms are real. Always.
14. A beer gut does not make you invisible to the opposite sex.
15. Guys in hockey masks don't attack you.
16. You don't have to lug a bag of useless stuff around everywhere you go.
17. People expect you to masturbate.

18. You can go to the bathroom without a support group.
19. Your last name stays put.
20. You can leave a hotel bed unmade.
21. When your work is criticized, you don't have to panic that everyone secretly hates you.
22. You can kill your own food.
23. The garage is all yours.
24. You get extra credit for the slightest act of thoughtfulness.
25. You can fart with impunity.
26. Nobody secretly wonders if you swallow.
27. You never have to clean the toilet. Or oven. Or floor.
28. You can be showered and ready in 10 minutes.
29. Sex means never worrying about your reputation.
30. Wedding plans take care of themselves.
31. If someone forgets to invite you to something, he or she can still be your friend.
32. Your underwear is $5 for a three pack.
33. You understand why Beavis and Butt-head is funny.

34. None of your co-workers have the power to make you cry.

35. You don't have to shave below your neck.

36. You don't have to curl up next to a hairy guy every night.

37. If you're 34 and single nobody gives a shit.

38. You can write your name in the snow.

39. You don't have to bother having a proper conversation with your mates down at the pub.

40. Everything on your face stays its original color.

41. You never have to make your bed.

42. You understand the offside rule.

43. You can quietly enjoy a car ride from the passenger seat.

44. Flowers fix everything.

45. You never have to worry about other people's feelings, or see 44 above.

46. You get to think about sex 90% of your waking hours.

47. You can wear a white shirt in the rain.

48. Three pair of shoes are more than enough for most of your life.

49. You can boast about the number of people you've slept with.

50. You can say anything and not worry about what people think.

51. You can eat dinner with just a knife.

52. Michael Bolton doesn't live in your universe.

53. Nobody stops telling a good dirty joke when you walk into the room.

54. You can whip your shirt off on a hot day.

55. You don't have to clean your house if the meter reader is coming by.

56. If your friend leaves the bar with a new girl it's OK.

57. Car mechanics tell you the truth.

58. You don't give a shit if no one notices your new haircut.

59. You can watch a game in silence with your room mate for hours without even thinking "He must be mad at me"

60. Sentences have only one meaning.

61. You never misconstrue innocuous statements to mean your lover is about to leave you.

62. You can play and enjoy computer games other than Tetris.

63. Hot wax never comes near your pubic area.

64. One mood, all the time.
65. You never have to empty the dishwasher.
66. You remember the punch lines to jokes.
67. You know at least a dozen ways to open a beer bottle.
68. You can sit with your knees apart no matter what you are wearing.
69. Haircuts are $12.
70. Grey hair adds character.
71. You can never lose half your bathing suit.
72. You can wear sneakers to a wedding.
73. You don't care if someone is talking about you behind your back.
74. With 400 million sperm per shot, you could double the Earth's population in 15 tries, at least in theory.
75. You don't have to try other people's desserts.
76. Curse words don't bother you.
77. The remote is yours.
78. You get to drive most of the time.
79. You can sit in a pub on your own without jerkoffs trying to pick you up.
80. You can drop by to see a friend without bringing a little gift.
81. Stag nights are much more fun than Hen nights.

82. You have a normal and healthy relationship with your mother.

83. You can buy condoms without the shop-keeper imagining you naked.

84. You needn't pretend you're "freshening up" to go to the toilet.

85. If you don't call your buddy when you say you will, he won't tell your friends you've changed.

86. Someday you'll be a dirty old man.

87. You can rationalise any behavior with the handy phrase "Fuck it!"

88. If an other guy shows up at the party in the same outfit, neither of you care.

89. You can teach your friend's children swear words.

90. The occasional well-rendered belch is practically expected.

91. You never have to miss a sexual opportunity because you're not in the mood.

92. You think the idea of punting a small dog is funny.

93. If something mechanical didn't work, you can bash it with a hammer and throw it across the room.

96. You don't have to remember everyone's birthdays and anniversaries.

97. You can't get pregnant.

98. Wrinkles add character

99. You can "do" your nails with a pocket knife

100. You are unable to see wrinkles in your clothes

101. You are not expected to know the names of more than five colors

102. You have more than one way to spell most words.

103. If you mess up, you can just say "Hey, I fucked up!" and kinda leave it at that.

How Manly are you?
A quick 10-Question test:

1. In the company of females, intercourse should be referred to as:
   A. Lovemaking
   B. Screwing
   C. Taking the pigskin bus to tuna town.

2. You should make love to a woman for the first time only after you've both shared:
   A. Your views about what you expect from a sexual relationship.
   B. Your blood-test results.
   C. Five tequila slammers.

3. You time your orgasm so that:
   A. Your partner climaxes first.
   B. You both climax simultaneously.
   C. You don't miss ESPN Sportscenter.

4. Passionate, spontaneous sex on the kitchen floor is:
   A. Healthy, creative love-play.
   B. Not the sort of thing your wife/girlfriend would agree to.
   C. Not the sort of thing your wife/girlfriend needs to ever find out about.

5. Spending the whole night cuddling a woman you've just had sex with is:
A. The best part of the experience.
B. The second best part of the experience.
C. $100 extra.

6. Your girlfriend says she's gained five pounds in the last month. You tell her that it is:
A. No concern of yours.
B. Not a problem, she can join your gym.
C. A conservative estimate.

7. You think today's sensitive, caring man is:
A. A myth
B. An oxymoron
C. A moron

8. Foreplay is to sex as:
A. Appetizer is to entree.
B. Primer is to paint.
C. A long line is to an amusement park ride.

9. Which of the following are you most likely to find yourself saying at the end of a relationship?

A. "I hope we can still be friends."

B. "I'm not in right now, please leave a message at the beep."

C. "That was great. I'll come back again next year."

10. A woman who is uncomfortable watching you masturbate:

A. Probably needs a little more time before she can cope with that sort of intimacy.

B. Is uptight and a waste of time.

C. Shouldn't have sat next to you on the plane in the first place.

If you answered "A" more than 7 times, check your pants to make sure you really are a man.

If you answered "B" more than 7 times, check into therapy, you're a little confused.

If you answered "C" more than 7 times, "YOU ARE A MANLY MAN!"

PMS

THE TOP 14 THINGS PMS STANDS FOR

Pass My Shotgun
Psychotic Mood Shift
Perpetual Munching Spree
Puffy Mid-Section
People Make Me Sick
Provide Me with Sweets
Pardon My Sobbing
Pimples May Surface
Pass My Sweatpants
Pissy Mood Syndrome
Plainly; Men Suck
Pack My Stuff
Permanent Menstrual Syndrome

Reality: They call it PMS because Mad Cow Disease was already taken...

DANGEROUS PMS STATEMENTS MEN MAKE

Dangerous: What's for dinner?
  SAFER: Can I help you with dinner?
  SAFEST: Where would you like to go for
    dinner?

DANGEROUS: Are you wearing THAT?
  SAFER: Gee, you look good in brown.
  SAFEST: Wow! Look at you!

DANGEROUS: What are you so worked up
    about?
  SAFER: Could we be overreacting?
  SAFEST: Here's fifty dollars.

DANGEROUS: Should you be eating that?
  SAFER: You know, there are a lot of apples
    left.
  SAFEST: Can I get you a glass of wine with
    that?

DANGEROUS: What did you DO all day?
  SAFER: I hope you didn't overdo it today.
  SAFEST: I've always loved you in that robe.

Quotations about Women

Quotations about Women

Here's to women, if we could only fall into their arms — without falling into their hands.
Ambrose Bierce

Quotations about Women

A woman is only a woman, but a good cigar is a smoke.
Rudyard Kipling

More Quotations about Women

If a woman likes another woman, she's cordial. If she doesn't like her, she's very cordial.
Irvin S. Cobb

Still More Quotes About Women

Let us have wine and women, mirth and lafter, sermons and soda water the day after.
Lord Byron

Some people like women... Quotes

Men, some to pleasure, some to business take, but every woman is at heart a rake.
Alexander Pope

Some people don't...

Next to the wound, what women make best is the bandage.
Barbey d'Aurevilly
Some people have mixed feelings.

A true gentlemen is one who is never unintentionally rude.
Oscar Wilde
Sayings about Men

When thou goest to woman, take thy whip.
Friedrich Nietzsche
These people are tough on women

All tragedies are finished by a death,
All comedies are ended by a marriage.
Lord Byron
Quotations about Marriage

In the election of a wife as in a project of war, to err but once is to be undone forever.
Thomas Middleton
Wives

Apparently, the way to a girl's heart is to saw her in half.
Victor Mature
Famous People Quotations

You call this a party? The beer is warm and the women are cold!
Groucho Marx
Movie Quotations about Women

The years that a woman subtracts from her age are not lost. They are added onto the ages of other women.
Deane de Poitiers
Quotes from Women, on Women

Never trust a woman who tells her real age. A woman who would tell one that would tell one anything.
Oscar Wilde

Advice

A woman always has her revenge ready.
Moliere Warningser

Warnings

"Here's to woman - if only we could fall into their arms — without falling into their hands."
Ambrose Bierce

Quotations About Women

"A lady is one who never shows her underwear unintentionally."
Lillian Day, Kiss and Tell

"All women are the same when the lights are out."
Plutarch, Essey

"Nothing is more unbearable than a woman of wealth."
Juvenal, Satires, Sat.VI, 1. 460

"Women are silver dishes into which we put golden apples."
Goether, Conversations with Echermann

"Were it not for gold and women, there would be no damnation."
Cyril Tourneur, Revengers Tragedy

"Two women placed together makes cold weather."
Henry VIII Act 1 Sc 4 l.22

"Were there no women, men might live like Gods."
Dekker, Honest Whore Pt.1 ActIII Sc.1

"You sometimes have to answer a woman according to her womanishness, just as you have to answer a fool according to his folly."
Bernard Shaw,
Unsocial Socialist Ch. XVIII

"She knifed me one night 'cause I wished she was white, and I learned about women from 'er."
Rudyard Kipling, The Ladies

"When I say that I don't know women, I mean that I know that I don't know them. Every single woman I ever knew is a puzzle to me, as I have no doubt she is to herself."
James Makepeace Thackeray,
Mrs. Brown's Letters

"Money can't buy love, but it improves your bargaining position."
L. J. Peter

"I expect that woman will be the last thing civilized by man."
George Meredith,
The Ordeal of Richard Feverel I

"Sensible and responsible women do not want to vote. The relative positions to be assumed by man and woman in the working out of our civilization were assigned long ago by a higher intelligence than ours."
Grover Cleveland,
Ladies Home Journal, April 1905

"A ship and a woman are ever needing repair."
George Herbert, Jacula Prudentum

"Any mechanism hard to manage is usually feminine."
Miles Abbott

"Anatomy is Destiny."
Sigmund Freud

"All women become like their mothers. That is their tragedy."
Oscar Wilde

"Let the woman learn in silence with all subjection. But I suffer not a woman to teach, nor to usurp authority over the man, but to be in silence."
The Bible 11 Timothy 2:11

"Who can find a virtuous woman? For her price is far above rubies."
Proverbs, 31:10

~ The Danielle Adams Publishing Company ~

"A woman is only a woman, but a good cigar is a smoke."
Rudyard Kipling, The Betrothed

More Quotations About Women

"Women have no rank."
Napoleon

"The trouble with women is that they lack the power of conversation but not the power of speech."
George Bernard Shaw

"Like all young men, you greatly exaggerate the difference between one young woman and another."
George Bernard Shaw, Major Barbara, Act III

"Widow, like ripe fruit, drop easily from their perch."
Jean de La Bruyere

"Virtue is learned at mothers knee, vice at other joints."
L.J. Peter

"Failing to be there when a man wants her is a woman's greatest sin, except to be there when he doesn't want her."
Helen Rowland

(Women) The weaker vessel.
New Testament, I Peter 3,7

"Despite my 30 years of research into the feminine soul, I have not yet been able to answer... the great question that has never been answered: What does a woman want?"
Sigmund Freud

"The happiest women, like the happiest nations, have no history."
George Eliot,
The Mill on the Floss, book 6

"A little while she strove and much repented, and whispering I will ne'er consent, consented."
George Gorden, Lord Byron,
Don Juan

"And the best and the worst of this
Is that neither is most to blame,
If you have forgotten my kisses
And I have forgotten your name."
  An Interlude,
  Algernon Charles Swinburne

"Woman indeed was born of delay itself."
  Plautus Miles Gloriosus

Two women in one house, two cats and one mouse, two dogs and one bone, may never accord in one home.
  Anon

"Do you not know I am a woman, when I think I must speak."
  Shakespeare, As You Like It Ch 3 sc 2

"Man's love is of man's life a thing apart, 'tis woman's whole existence."
  Lord Byron Don Juan st. 194

"A French woman, when double crossed, will kill her rival; An Italian woman would rather kill her deceitful lover; and an Englishwoman simply breaks off relations - but they all will console themselves with another man."

Charles Boyer

"A woman is never quite as old as her dearest friend says she is."

L. J. Peter

"To the woman He said, 'I will multiply your pain in child bearing; in pain you shall bring forth children yet your desire shall be for your husband, and he shall rule over you.'"

The Bible (Genesis 3:16)

"A society in which women are taught anything but the management of a family, the care of men, and the creation of the future generation is a society which is on the way out."

L. Ron Hubbard

"If a woman hasn't got a tiny streak of a harlot in her, she's a dry stick as a rule."
D.H. Lawrence,
Pornography and Obscenity,
this Quarter, 1929

"If the queen had any balls, she'd be king."
William Makepeace Thackeray

"This book is not to be tossed aside lightly - it should be thrown with great force!"
Dorothy Parker

*"If a woman likes another woman,
   she's cordial.
If she doesn't like her, she's very cordial."*
   Irvin S. Cobb

Still More Quotations About Women

"A beautiful woman should break her mirror early."
   Baltasar Gracian

"Behind every successful man you'll find a woman who has nothing to wear."
   Harold Coffin

"In order that the lists of able women may be memorized for use at meetings of the opposed sex, Heaven has considerately made it brief."
   Ambrose Bierce

When asked to state a broad rule for avoiding Congressional sex scandals: "The broad rule is that broads ought to be able to type."
   James Wright

"After 40, a woman needs a lover and a good face lift. After 50, cash."
Austine Hearst

"Give a woman a job and she grows balls."
Jack Gelber

"I do not like women who meddle
   with politics."
Napoleon Bonaparte to Madame de Condorcet

"All the great pleasures in life are silent."
Georges Clemenceau

"If we are to judge love by it's consequences, it more nearly resembles hatred than friend-ship."
La Rochefoucauld

"Were it not for imagination, a man would be as happy in the arms of a chambermaid as of a duchess."
Samuel Johnson

"You don't have to deserve your mother's love.
You have to deserve your father's. He's more
particular."
   Robert Frost

"I know the nature of women;
When you want to, they don't want to;
And when you don't want to, they desire
exceedingly."
   Terence

"Whether they give or refuse, all women are
glad to have been asked."
   Ovid

"Even the cleverest woman finds need for foolish admirers." Anon

"Though statisticians in our time
have never kept the score
Man wants a great deal here
And women even more."
   James Thurber

"Let us have wine and women, mirth and lafter, Sermons and soda water the day after."
Lord Byron

These People Like Women

"There are three faithful friends: an old wife, an old dog, and ready money."
Ben Franklin

"Wives are young men's mistresses, companions for middle age, and old men's nurses."
Francis Bacon

"In every mess I find a friend, in every port a wife."
Charles Dibdin, Jack in his Element

"The two divinest things this world has got, A lovely woman in a rural spot!"
Leigh Hunt, the story of Rimini

"I like clean ladies and nice ladies."
Lawrence Welk, Playboy 1979

"Men, some to business, some to pleasure take, but every woman is at heart a rake."
Alexander Pope

These People Don't like Women

Two women are worse than one.
Plautus, Curculio Act V, Sc. 1

God created man and, finding him not suffi-ciently alone, gave him a companion to make him feel his solitude more keenly.
Paul Valery, Tel Quel

All women be evils, yet necessary evils.
Brian Melbancke, Philotimus 1583

Women are the gate of Hell..
St. Jerome

Regard the society of women as a necessary unpleasantness of social life, and avoid it as much as possible.
Tolstoy, Diary entry

Women, deceived by men, want to marry them. It is a revenge, as good as any other.
Phillippe De Remibeaumanoir

If it came down to the choice between a woman and a radio, I'd choose the radio. It brings the outside world in.
Eldridge Cleaver

Friendship among women is only a suspension of hostilities
Comte de Rivarol 1753 - 1801

All women are sirens at heart.
Earnst Lubitsch

"Oh woman, perfect woman! What distraction was meant to mankind with thou made as a devil. What an inviting hell invented."
Francis Baumont, Comedy of Monsuir Thomans

"A woman should be seen and not heard."
Sophocles 495-406 B.C.

"Oh woman, woman, when to ill thy mind is bent all hell contains no fouler fiend."
Homer, The Oddesy

"Trust a woman? I'll trust the devil first."
John Fletcher

"Next to the wound, what women make best is the bandage."
Barbvey d'Aurevilly

These People Have Mixed Emotions about Women

"Woman is at once apple and serpent."
Heinrich Heine

"There are two tragedies in life. One is to not get your heart's desire. The other is to get it."
Man and Superman, George Bernard Shaw

"To be slow in words is a woman's only virtue."
Shakespeare, Two Gentlemen of Verona,
Act III Sc. 1 L. 338

"There was a little girl
Who had a little curl
Right in the middle of he forehead,
When she was good
She was very, very good,
But when she was bad she was horrid."
Henry Wadsworth Longfellow
B.R.T. Machetta, Home Life of Longfellow.

"When the candles are out all women are fair."
Plutarch, Conjugal Precepts

"Patience makes a woman beautiful in middle age."
Elliot Paul

"Unless a woman has an amorous heart, she is a dull companion."
Samuel Johnson 1709 - 1784

"Silence gives grace to a woman."
Sophocles, Ajax L. 293

"Be plain in dress, and sober in your diet;
In short, my deary, kiss me, and be quiet."
Lady Mary Wortley Montagu,
A summary of Lord Lyttelton's advice

"I am very fond of the company of ladies. I like their beauty, I like their delicacy, I like their vivacity, I like their silence."
Samuel Johnson,
Seward's Johnsoniana

"Does the imagination dwell the most upon a woman won or a woman lost?"
William Butler Yeats, The Tower

"They have an entertaining tattle, and sometimes wit, but for solid reasoning, good sense, I never new in my life one that had it, or who reasoned or acted consequentially for four and twenty hours together."
Rudyard Kipling

"Women - you can't live with them, you can't live without them."
Aristophanes, Lysistrata

"Women - you can't live with them, and you can't shoot them."
M. Manly

"A true gentlemen is one who is never unintentionally rude."
Oscar Wilde

Quotations about Men

"A man is as old as he's feeling,
A woman as old as she looks."
Mortimer Collins -
The Unknown Quantity

"The best way to hold a man is in your arms."
Mae West

"A man who won't lie to a woman has very little consideration for her feelings."
Olin Miller

"A man's desire is for the woman; but the woman's desire is rarely other than for the desire of the man."
Samuel Taylor Coleridge

"Women were created for the comfort of men."
Howell, Familiar Letters: to Sargent D

"A little inaccuracy saves a world of explanation."
C.E. Ayres

"Woman may be said to be an inferior man."
Aristotle, Poetics XV

"If you resolve to give up smoking, drinking, and women, you don't actually live longer; it just seems longer."
Clement Freud

"No one in this world needs a mink coat but a mink." Anon.

"Love, and do what you like."
Saint Augustine

"A gentlemen is one who wouldn't hit a woman with his hat on."
Fred Allen

"Wherever I travel, I'm too late. The orgy has moved elsewhere."
Mordecai Richler

"No man is lonely while eating spaghetti - it requires so much attention."
Christopher Morely

"Whatever women do they must do twice as well as men to be thought half as good. Luckily, this is not difficult."
Charlotte Wittleton.

"Charlotte Wittleton is a bitch."
Dr. Man

"A man's idee in a card game is war - crool, devastatin' and pitiless. A lady's idee iv it is a combynation iv larceny, embezzlement an' burglary."
Finley Peter Dunne

"A man in love is incomplete until he has married. Then he's finished."
Zsa Zsa Gabor

"A man is a person who will pay two dollars for a one dollar item he wants. A woman will pay one dollar for a two dollar item she doesn't want."
William Binger

"The bit of truth behind all this - one so eagerly denied - is that men are not gentle, friendly creatures wishing for love, who simply defend themselves if they are attacked, but that a powerful measure of desire for aggression has to be reckoned as part of their instinctual endowment."

Sigmund Freud - Civilization and its Discontents

"The right to be let alone is the most comprehensive of rights and the right most valued in civilized man."

Justice Louis D. Brandeis

"When thou goest to woman, take thy whip."
Friedrich Nietzsche

Tough. These people are tough on women.

"There is no worse evil than a bad woman."
Euripides 480 bc

"A woman, an ass, a walnut tree
Bring the more fruit the more beaten they be."
Guazzo, Civil Conversation (1586)

"For men at most differ as Heaven and Earth,
But women, worst and best, as Heaven and
Hell."
*Tennyson, Idylls of the King,
Merlin and Vivian*

"She's the sort of woman who lives for others
- you can tell the others by their hunted expres-
sion."
C.S. Lewis the Screwtape letters

"Half the sorrows of women would be averted
if they could repress the speech they know to
be useless."
George Eliot in Felix Holt

"The only reason I am glad that I am a woman is that I will not have to marry one."
Ida M. Tarbell

"A dead woman bites not."
Patrick, 6th Lord Gray
(Gray advocated the execution of Mary, Queen of Scotts. 1587 (Whew! This guy was really tough!)

"For the study of the good and bad in woman two women are a needless expense."
Ambrose Bierce: Epigram

"Gin was mother's milk to her."
George Bernard Shaw,
Pygmalion Act III

"Man's inhumanity to man is only exceeded by woman's inhumanity to woman."
Percy Forman

"When Eve first saw her reflection in a pool, she sought Adam and accused him of infidelity."
Ambrose Bierce

"Woman may be said to be an inferior man."
   Aristotle

"I judge impetuosity to be better than caution; for Fortune is a woman, and if you wish to master her, you must strike and beat her."
   Niccolo Machiavelli, The Prince

"Anyone who knows anything of history knows that the great social changes are impossible without the feminine ferment. Social progress can be measured exactly by the social position of the fair sex - the ugly ones included."
   Karl Marx, Letter 1868

**"All tragedies are finish'd by a death,
all comedies are ended by a marriage."**
Lord Byron

Marriage

"Marriage: A sort of friendship recognized by the police."
Robert Louis Stevenson

"An end of many short follies - being one long stupidity."
Nietzsche

"A man finds himself seven years older the day after his marriage."
Francis Bacon

"Marriage is neither heaven or hell, it is simply purgatory."
Abraham Lincoln

"We wedded men live in sorrow."
Chaucer

"I got married, and we had a baby nine months and ten seconds later."
Jane Mansfield

"To the question when a man should marry? 'A young man not yet, an elder man not at all."
Francis Bacon 1561-1626

Sharper: "Thus grief still treads upon the heels of pleasure:
Marry'd in haste, we may repent at leisure."
Setter: "Some by experience find those words mis-plac'd;
At leisure marry'd, they repent in haste."
William Congreve,
The Old Bachelor V. ix

"It goes far toward reconciling me to being a woman when I reflect that I am thus in no danger of marrying one."
Lady Mary Wortley Montagu

"It is a woman's business to get married as soon as possible, and a man's to keep unmarried as long as he can."
George Bernard Shaw

"Many a good hanging prevents a bad marriage."
Shakespeare. Twelfth Night v, (20)

"American women seek in their husbands a perfection which English women seek only in their butlers."
Oscar Wilde

"Marriage is the alliance of two people. One of whom never remembers birthdays and the other whom never forgets."
Ogden Nash

"Of two kinds of temporary insanity, one ends in suicide, the other in marriage."
Ambrose Bierce

"Married men make very poor husbands."
Frank Crowninshield, Vanity Fair

"Marriage, to tell the truth, is an evil, but a necessary evil."
Menander 324 B.C.

"As to marriage or celibacy, let a man take which course he will, he will be sure to repent."
Socrates

"All aught to refrain from a marriage who cannot avoid abject poverty for their children."
Charles Darwin,
The Descent of Man

"A system could not well have been devised more studiously hostile to human happiness than marriage."
Percy Bysshe Shelley,
Queen Mab, Notes, 1813

"Marriage: A long conversation checkered by disputes."
Robert Louis Stevenson

"One should always be in love. That is the reason one should never marry."
Oscar Wild

"Marriage: putting one's hand into a bag of snakes on the chance of drawing out an eel."
Leonardo da Vinci

"A man may be a fool and not know it, but not if he is married."
H.L. Mencken

"No matter how happily a woman may be married, it always pleases her to discover that there is a nice man who wishes she were not."
  H.L. Mencken

"There is nothing that so much seduces reason from vigilance as the thought of passing life with an amiable woman."
  Samuel Johnson;
    Letter to Joseph Baretti, 1762

"Any married man should forget his mistakes - no use two people remembering the same thing."
  Duane Dewel

"Grandchildren don't make a man feel old, it's the knowledge he's married to a grandmother."
  Norman Collie

"Marriage from love, like vinegar from wine -
A sad, sour, sober, beverage - by time
Is sharpen'd from its high celestial flavour,
Down to a very homely household savour."
  c. III. st. 5 Shakespeare

"Oh! How many torments lie in the small circle of a wedding ring."
Balzac

"Bachelors know more about women than married men; if they didn't, they'd be married too."
H.L. Mencken

"A young man married is a man that's marred. All's well that ends well." iii.
Shakespeare [315]

"In the election of a wife as in a project of war, to err but once is to be undone forever."
Thomas Middleton,
Anything for a Quiet Life, Act 1 Sc.1

Wives

"A wife has a lot of nerve expecting her husband to be faithful when she gets old and fat."
Groucho Marx

"Evil comes to us men of the imagination wearing as it's mask all the virtues. I have certainly known more men destroyed by the desire to have a wife and child and to keep them in comfort than I have seen destroyed by drink and harlots."
William Butler Yeats

"A good marriage would be between a blind wife and a deaf husband."
Michel de Montaigne 1533-1592

"There is no fury like an ex-wife searching for a new lover."
Cyril Connolly -
The Uniquiet Grave Part I

"Ne'er take a wife till thou hast a house, and a fire to put her in."
Benjamin Franklin

"He that hath wife and children hath given hostages to fortune, for they are impediments to great enterprises, either of virtue or mischief."
Francis Bacon
Of Marriage and the Single Life

"Mothers, wives, and maids,
There be the tools wherewith priests manage men."
Robert Browning in
The Ring and the Book, iv

"Women should remain at home, sit still, keep house, and bear and bring up children."
Martin Luther

**"Apparently, the way to a girl's heart
is to saw her in half."**
Victor Mature

Famous People Quotes

"Women are like elephants. They're nice to
look at but I wouldn't want to own one."
W.C Fields

"I have an intense desire to return to the
womb. Anybody's."
Woody Allen

"Many a man has fallen in love with a girl in a
light so dim he would not have chosen a suit
by it."
Maurice Chevalier

"My interest in the cinema has lapsed since
women began to talk."
George J. Nathan

"Daddy warned me about drinking and men,
but he never said anything about women and
drugs."
Tallulah Bankhead

"The trouble with life is that there are so many beautiful women - and so little time!"
John Barrymore

"It was a woman who drove me to drink - and, you know, I never even thanked her."
W.C. Fields

"I know a lot of people didn't expect our relationship to last - but we've just celebrated our two month's anniversary."
Britt Ekland

"When I am married, I want to be single, and when I am single, I want to be married."
Cary Grant

"The rest of my life will be devoted to women and litigation."
Errol Flynn

"Working in Hollywood does give one a certain expertise in the field of prostitution."
Jane Fonda

"If you don't have an orgasm daily, you become very nervous, very uptight. I do, anyway."
Linda Lovelace

"From Childhood I was told never to marry a gentile woman, never to shave on Saturday, and most especially never to shave a gentile woman on Saturday."
Woody Allen

"I always said I won't marry until I go to Japan and see the beautiful women there. I've been to Japan now, and I have to have another excuse."
Maximilian Schell

"There are three things a woman can make out of almost nothing - a salad, a hat, and a quarrel."
John Barrymore

"Gals are super, But I haven't changed my opinion of them: I still like them best in the bedroom and the kitchen."
Bobby Riggs

"Why don't you sit on my lap when we're discussing your contract - the way the other girls do?"
Louis B. Mayer

"The only position for women in the movement is prone."
Stokely Carmichael

"I don't object to a woman doing anything in combat as long as she gets home in time to cook dinner!"
Barry Goldwater

*"It's not as easy to get laid as it used to be.
Ya' think a girl goes for you and you find out
a girl is going after your money or your balls.
Or your money and your balls."*
Jack Nicholson, Carnal Knowledge

Movie Quotes

"There's a name for you ladies, but it isn't used
in high society - outside of a kennel.
Joan Crawford in "The Women"

"Even as a kid, I always went for the wrong
women. I feel that's my problem. When my
mother took me to see Snow White, everyone
fell in love with Snow White. I immediately
fell for the wicked queen."
Woody Allen, Annie Hall

"Drunk! I'll have you know a Harvard man
never resorts to getting a woman drunk -- except in an emergency. And you, Miss Morrow,
are an emergency."
*Nick Adams to Doris Day
in 'Pillow Talk'*

"I don't know what women get so mad about, they control half the money, and all the pussy."
From the movie D.C. Cab

"She tried to sit on my lap...While I was standing up!"
Humphrey Bogart describing Martha Vickers in the "Big Sleep"

"The chances are you'll get off with life. That means if you're a good girl, you'll be out in 20 years. I'll be waiting for you. If they hang you, I'll always remember you."
Humphrey Bogart to Mary Astor in The Maltese Falcon

"I wish I had your confidence. I've never been able to discover an honest warmth in any woman."
Leo Genn to Robert Taylor in Quo Vadis

"The women. How much for the women?
John Belushi in the Blues Brothers

"Remember: You're fighting for this woman's honor, which is probably more than she ever did."
> *Groucho Marx, insulting*
> *Margaret Dumont in 'Duck Soup'*

"There is no sincerity like a woman telling a lie."
> *Cecil Parket describing*
> *Ingrid Bergman in Indiscreet*

"Women should not think at all. They are not equal to it."
> *Robert Brice to his brother in*
> *Dragon Seed.*

"Women should be kept illiterate and clean, like canaries."
> *Roscoe Karns expressing an opinion*
> *in Woman of the Year.*

"Certain women should be struck regularly, like gongs."
> *Robert Montgomery*
> *in Private Lives.*

"Marriage is a dull meal, with the dessert at the beginning."
Jose Ferrer in Moulin Rouge

"Jonathan, before a man gets married, he's a - he's like a tree in the forest. He, he stands there independent, an entity unto himself. And then he's chopped down. His branches are cut off, he's stripped of his bark, and he's thrown into the river with the rest of the logs. Then this tree is taken to the mill. Now when it comes out, it's not longer a tree, It's the vanity table, the breakfast nook, the baby crib, and the newspaper that lines the family garbage can."
Tony Randall receiving bachelorhood information in 'Pillow Talk'

"Damn Mrs. Pearce! And Damn the Coffee! And damn you! And damn my own folly in having lavished hard earned knowledge and the treasure of my regard and intimacy on a heartless guttersnipe."
*Leslie Howard telling off
Wendy Hiller in Pygmalion*

"Frankly, my dear, I don't give a damn."
Clark Gable walking out
on Vivien Leigh in Gone With the Wind

"You call this a party?
The beer is warm, and the women are cold."
Groucho Marx in Monkey Business

"Why don't you get out of that wet coat, and
into a dry martini?"
Robert Benchlet to Ginger Rogers in
The Major and the Minor.

"The only time a woman doesn't talk is when
she's dead."
Wm Demarest,
in The Miracle of Morgan's Creek

"They all start out as Juliets and wind up as
Lady Macbeths."
William Holden speculating
in The Country Girl

"Women, as some witty Frenchman put it, in-
spire us with the desire to do masterpieces and
always prevent us from carrying them out."
George Sanders
in Picture of Dorian Gray

"I thought you were sexless, but you've suddenly turned into a woman. Do you know how I know that? Because you, not me, are taking pleasure in my being tied up. All women, whether they want to face it or not, want to see a man in a tied up situation. They spend their whole lives trying to get a man into a tied up situation. Their lives are fulfilled when they can get a man - or as many men as they can - into a tied up situation."
    Richard Burton to Deborah Kerr in
    Night of the Iguana

"See what happens today? Women want to act like men and want to be treated like women."
    Gene Kelly, An American in Paris

The years that a woman subtracts from her age are not lost.
They are added to the ages of other women.
Deane de Poitiers

Quotes by Women

"I never hated a man enough to give his diamonds back."
Zsa Zsa Gabor

"All women's dresses are merely variations on the external struggle between the admitted desire to dress and the unadmitted desire to undress."
Lin Yutang

"The only question left to be settled now is, are women persons?"
Susan B. Anthony

"Women's virtue is man's greatest invention."
Cornelia Otis Skinner

"If a woman has the misfortune of knowing anything, she should conceal it as well as she can."
Jane Austen

"Women marry because they don't want to work."
Mary Garden

"God, for two people to be able to live together for the rest of their lives is almost unnatural."
Jane Fonda

"What is woman? Only one of nature's agreeable blunders."
Hannah Cowley, Who's the Dupe? Act II 2

"A husband is what's left of a man after the nerve is extracted."
Helen Rowland

"The Queen is most anxious to enlist every one who can   speak or write to join in checking this mad, wicked folly of "Women's Rights", with all its attendant horrors."
Queen Victoria
  Letter to Sir Theodore Martin
  29 May 1870

"You don't know a woman until you have had a letter from her."
Ada Leverson

"From birth to age 18, a girl needs good parents. From 18 to 35, she needs good looks. From 35 to 55 she needs a good personality. From 55 on, she needs good cash."
Sophie Tucker

"Even the most respectable woman has a complete set of clothes in her wardrobe ready for a possible abduction."
Sacha Guitry

"It's a terrible thing to say but I can't think of any good women writers."
Dorothy Parker

Reporting on a Yale Prom: "If all those sweet young things present were laid end to end... I wouldn't be a bit surprised."
Dorothy Parker

"I sometimes give myself admirable advice but I am incapable of taking it."
Lady Mary Wortley Montague, 1689-1762

"Girls who put out are tramps. Girls who don't are ladies. This is, however, a rather archaic usage of the word. Should one of you boys happen upon a girl who doesn't put out, do not jump to the conclusion that you have found a lady. What you have probably found is a lesbian."
Fran Lebowitz, Metropolitan Life

"It isn't tying himself to one woman that a man dreads when he thinks of marrying; it's separating himself from all the others."
Helen Rowland

"I am glad I am not a man, for if I were I should be obliged to marry a woman."
Mme de Stael

"You have too luscious a bosom to keep the conversation general."
Madame Armand (to a young wife who would open a salon.)

"Women have no sympathy... And my experience of women is almost as large as Europe. And it is so intimate too. ...No woman has excited passions among women more than I have."
Florence Nightingale, Letters to Madame Mohl

"[Breasts] are not parts of a person but lures slung around her neck, to be kneaded and twisted like magic, putty, or mumbled and mouthed like lolly ices."
Germaine Greer,
The Female Eunuch

"I always say that a girl never really looks as well as she does on board a steamship, or even a yacht."
Anita Loos,
Gentlemen Prefer Blonds

"If I have to, I can do anything. I am strong, I am invincible, I am woman."
Helene Ready

"Dear Helene: Can you stand up and write your name in the snow when you take a leak?"
Dr. Man

*One should never trust a woman
who tells her real age.
A woman who would tell one that
would tell one anything.*
Oscar Wilde

ADVICE

"A woman's advice has little value, but he who won't take it is a fool."
Cervantes: Don Quixote II.7

"A man's only weapon against a woman is his hat. He should grab it and run."
Damon Runyon

"Never forget to assure a woman that she is unlike any other woman in the world, which she will believe, after which you may proceed to deal with her as any other woman in the world."
D.B. Wyndham Lewis

"Advice to persons about to marry - "Don't.'"
Punch vol viii, p.1. 1845

"The only way a man can get the better of a woman in an argument is to let her keep on talking after she has won it."
Richard Attridge

"It is better to dwell in the wilderness than with a contentious and angry woman."
Proverbs 21;19

"Tis better to have loved and lost, than never to have lost at all."
Samuel Butler

"The chance of a meaningful relationship with the member of the opposite sex is inversely proportional to their amount of beauty."
Sean Duffy

"Never eat in a place called Mom's. Never play cards with a man called Doc. And never lie down with a woman who's got more troubles than you."
Nelson Algren

"A used car is like a bad woman - no matter how good you treat it, it'll give you more trouble than it's worth."
William Makepeace Thackeray

"Certain women should be struck regularly, like gongs."
Noel Coward, Private lives III

"Verily the best women are those who are content with little."
Mohammed

"Remember, It's as easy to marry a rich woman as a poor woman."
William Makepeace Thackeray, Pendennis Ch. 28

"A woman friend! He who believes that weakness steers in a stormy night without a compass."
Fletcher, Woman Pleased Act II Sc, 1

Thank you for your purchase. To see our other books, please visit our website at www.danielleadams.com.

Published by -
~ THE DANIELLE ADAMS PUBLISHING CO. ~
BOX 100 ☆ MERION STATION, PA 19066
FAX 610/642-6832 ☆ VOICE 610/642-1000
©2012

All wickedness is but little
to the wickedness of a women.
Ecclesiasticus XXV 19

Warnings

"When towards the Devil's house we tread,
woman's a thousand steps ahead."
Goethe, Faust I.21.147

"O woman, woman when to ill thy mind is
bent, all hell contains no fouler fiend."
Homer, The Odyssey Book XXI L. 531

"Women and elephants never forget an injury."
H.H. Munro, Reginald on Besetting Sins

"A slighted woman knows no bounds."
John Vanbrugh, The Mistake Pt1, Act II Sc. 1

"Never confuse I love you with I want to marry
you."
Cleveland Amory

"I've seen your stormy seas and your stormy
women, and pity lovers rather more than sea-
men."
Byron, Don Juan

"Everything that deceives may be said to enchant."
Plato

"Educating a beautiful woman is like pouring honey on a fine swiss watch: everything stops."
Kurt Vonnegut

"He who wants a rose must respect the thorn."
Persian Proverb

"Heav'n has no rage like love to hatred turn'd,
Nor hell a fury like a woman scorn'd."
William Congreve, The Morning Bride Act III Sc. 8

"There is no excellent beauty that hath not some strangeness in the proportion of the beauty."
Francis Bacon

"In revenge and in love woman is more barbarous than man."
*Friedrich Wilhelm Nietzsche,
   Beyond Good and Evil*

"A woman always has her revenge ready."
Moliere (1622-73) Tartuffe Act1,i

"There are good marriages, but no delightful ones."
Duc De La Rochefoucauld

"If thee marries for money, thee surely will earn it."
Ezra Bowen

"As a jewel of gold in a swine's snout, so is a fair woman which is without discretion."
Old Testament, Proverbs 11, 22

"No woman is ever completely deceived."
Joseph Conrad, Under Western Eyes

Thank you for purchasing this book — we hope you have enjoyed it. We love women, yes even though they may have some faults — and we wouldn't want them any other way.

Addendum to Disclaimer. Continued from page 10.
By reading this text you agree to our 442 page agreement contract found on page 714 of our website, just like when you sign up for any mobile phone service or install any computer software. And this call is being recorded to bring you better service... yea — like recording the call had anything to do with bringing you better service. If we really wanted to bring you better service, we wouldn't record this call, and we'd have gotten rid of voice mail and answered the phone ourselves.

Anyhow, if you find a typo or misspelling in this book, we might have intentionally left a few in so you'd have something to point out to others—like you never had a typo in something you wrote—we appreciate your telling us so we can correct it in future editions. If you don't, it can no longer be considered our fault - we took a shot and spelled it the best way we could at the time. This policy falls in nicely with our disclaimer of responsibility as stated above.

We asked the writer to spell everything correctly and he replied "If you only have one way to spell a word, you're not really a man, are you?" That would explain the several different spelling variants of the same word in different chapters. Plus, try as we might, these mistakes just get out. We know you're not one of those really picky people who would hold it against us, are you? While you're standing there not doing anything, please take this book up to the cash register and purchase it. Thanks for buying this book. Or, as an alternative, just send us the money. Thank you.

Women: PS, if you are a woman trying to purchase this book, we advise against it - as it may contain material offensive to some readers. Please buy our book, "Life's too short to dance with short men." We love women, and we love to have a good time with them - and this book was written in fun but still, you probably won't enjoy it. It's not really written in spite — or "to get back at you" for making us put up with Hillary Clinton all these years. Really.

Thank you for your purchase.

We hope you enjoyed this title. If you are a woman and you were offended by these jokes and quotes - hey, don't look at us, we didn't originate them. It's like bashing a journalist for reporting a story of bad news. PLUS - We warned you in the front of the book not to read it. We can't help it if you can't follow instructions.

Take solace in Cosmo, Redbook, People, Soap Oprah Digest and Self magazines. You have your own little isle in the supermarket of stuff to read... so quit whining. Please buy our other titles including, "Life's Too Short to Dance with Short Men."

Sincerely,
Dr. Mann

Vital Signs

Vial Signs - over 100 very funny signs in a flip-style book.

A very, very funny sign book. All signs are one to a page and are about the size of a bumper sticker - flip to any page and display the funny sign of the day. Well, for the next hundred days, anyhow. Comes with a suction cup for affixing onto a car window, and has a built-in easel for standing on a counter or on your desk. Includes signs like:

· Keep Honking While I Reload

· Yes, I married Mr. Right... Mr. Always Right!

· Squirrels - Nature's Little Speed Bumps

· Horn Broken - Watch for Finger

· Of Course I Don't Look Busy - I did it right the first time!

· Men Have Feelings Too. Just Kidding.

· I didn't say it was your fault... I said I was going to blame you.

· I'm not blind. I'm ignoring you.

· A woman's favorite position? CEO.

· Helen Waite is now in charge of all RUSH orders -
    if you have a rush order please go to Helen Waite...

· If you don't like my driving, YOU come get these handcuffs off!"

· Hell Yes! I'm drunk - what do you think I am, a stunt driver?"

· Just blink if you want sex!

· Ring bell and run - the dog needs the exercise.

~ Pop-Out Easel ~
Stands book on desk or counter!
Display any sign - at any time!
Included FREE! Built right into each book!

Hang in Car Window!
Spiral Bound w/Hanger
Suction cup included, too!

"VITAL SIGNS"
~ Over 100 Priceless Sayings ~
Ready to Hang 'Most Anywhere: Car · Office · Home
Printed One Per Page - Ready to Display!

Vital signs is just $12.95 + $4 shipping and handling. We accept all major credit cards. Order two and include just $25 and the shipping is FREE! Order today by calling 610-642-1000! Or - order by mail - send check or credit card information to

The Danielle Adams Publishing Company
P.O. Box 100, Merion Station, PA 19066

Thank you - we print all our books
for our customers enjoyment! We do it all for you!

BOOKS

THEY'RE EVERYTHING
YOU'VE EVER IMAGINED...
AND MORE!

DANIELLE ADAMS
PUBLISHING COMPANY

Thank you for your purchase. To see our other books, please visit our website at www.danielleadams.com.

PUBLISHED BY -
~ THE DANIELLE ADAMS PUBLISHING CO. ~
BOX 100 ☆ MERION STATION, PA 19066
FAX 610/642-6832 ☆ VOICE 610/642-1000
©2012

CPSIA information can be obtained
at www.ICGtesting.com
Printed in the USA
BVOW06s0649310117
474854BV00031B/352/P